D1082763

BATTLES
THAT CHANGED THE WORLD

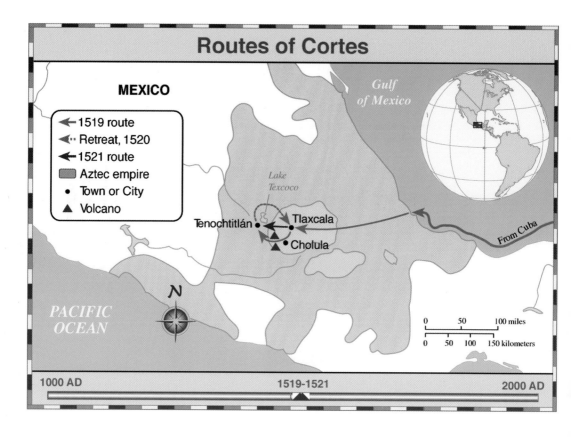

Routes of Cortes

MEXICO

Gulf of Mexico

1519 route
Retreat, 1520
1521 route
Aztec empire
Town or City
Volcano

Lake Texcoco

Tenochtitlán
Tlaxcala
Cholula

From Cuba

PACIFIC OCEAN

N

0   50   100 miles
0   50   100   150 kilometers

1000 AD   1519-1521   2000 AD

BATTLES
THAT CHANGED THE WORLD

TENOCHTITLAN

SAMUEL WILLARD CROMPTON

CHELSEA HOUSE PUBLISHERS
PHILADELPHIA

FRONTIS: The Aztec Empire was at its largest and most influential when the Spaniards landed in 1519. This map shows the routes Cortés and the Spaniards traveled during the siege of Tenochtitlan.

CHELSEA HOUSE PUBLISHERS

EDITOR IN CHIEF Sally Cheney
DIRECTOR OF PRODUCTION Kim Shinners
CREATIVE MANAGER Takeshi Takahashi
MANUFACTURING MANAGER Diann Grasse

STAFF FOR TENOCHTITLAN

ASSOCIATE EDITOR Bill Conn
PICTURE RESEARCHER Sarah Bloom
PRODUCTION ASSISTANT Jaimie Winkler
COVER AND SERIES DESIGNER Keith Trego
LAYOUT 21st Century Publishing and Communications, Inc.

©2002 by Chelsea House Publishers,
a subsidiary of Haights Cross Communications.
All rights reserved. Printed and bound in the United States of America.

http://www.chelseahouse.com

First Printing

1 3 5 7 9 8 6 4 2

Library of Congress Cataloging-in-Publication Data

Crompton, Samuel Willard.
    Tenochtitlan / Samuel Willard Crompton.
       v. cm.—(Battles that changed the world)
Includes index.
Contents: Year one—Two worlds, Aztec Mexico and Christian Spain—Parry and thrust: the Spanish advance to the Valley of Mexico—The Eighth of November: Montezuma and Cortâes meet—Uneasy coexistence—The night of sorrows—Building—Broken spears: the siege and destruction of Tenochtitlan—New Spain—Gods, men, animals and weapons.
    ISBN 0-7910-6681-9 (hardcover) — ISBN 0-7910-7166-9 (pbk.)
    1. Mexico—History—Conquest, 1519-1540—Juvenile literature. 2. Aztecs—History—Juvenile literature. [1. Mexico—History—Conquest,1519-1540. 2. Aztecs—History. 3. Indians of Mexico—History.] I. Title. II. Series.
F1230 .C945 2002

2002003770

CONTENTS

Year One Reed:
East Coast of Mexico,
Spring 1519

This Aztec stone relief shows the god Quetzacoatl—Aztec legends claimed he would return to restore harmony among his people. Many Aztecs initially believed Cortés and the Spaniards were messengers of Quetzacoatl, or perhaps even the god himself.

In order to ascertain what resemblance existed between the gold of the two countries, it would not be amiss to return it filled with grains of that metal, as a fit present for our emperor.

—Bernal Diaz,
The True History of the Conquest of Mexico

The strangers came early in the year One Reed. They came during the 20-day month the Aztecs called *Hueytozoztli,* which means "long watch." Strangers had come before, in the years Thirteen Rabbit and Twelve House, but they had left quickly each time. On this occasion the strangers intended to stay, rather than just visit.

The Aztecs watched as floating mountains seemed to appear off the shore. Clouds flew above these floating mountains. On the second day of their arrival, the strangers began to come ashore.

The strangers seemed like men, but of a different sort. Some Indians called them the "Ugly Ones" because of the hair on their faces. Other Indians feared that these men were gods, or at least the messengers of gods. If so, they were probably the messengers of the god *Quetzacoatl*, whose name means "Plumed Serpent."

Huge beasts, the likes of which had never been seen before, were lifted off the floating mountains. The beasts were then brought ashore in large canoes. There were other beasts too, snarling, ferocious animals.

In reality, the strange men that appeared on the beach that day were not gods, but Spanish explorers searching for gold. The floating mountains that brought them to Mexico were huge sailing ships, and the strange beasts, unknown to the Aztecs, were horses and dogs.

Thousands of Indians and hundreds of Spaniards met on the beach that day. Among them were four who held the keys to communication: Tentlil, Malinali, Aguilar, and Cortés.

Tentlil was the Aztec governor of the coastal region. His capital was at Cuelachtlan, about 15 miles away. For the past three days he had heard about the mysterious strangers on the beach, and now he had come to meet them. Tentlil was accompanied by about 4,000 of the Totonac people.

Malinali was a 15-year-old Mayan girl. She was born into a noble family, but had been sold into slavery when her mother and stepfather had a male child. They did not wish Malinali's birth rights to interfere with their new

Quetzacoatl

Quetzacoatl was a god of the Toltec people, who was adopted by the Aztecs after they settled in the Valley of Mexico. His name means "Plumed or Feathered Serpent."

Controversy surrounds Quetzacoatl. Some Aztec legends make him seem a hero-king, while others emphasize his divinity. It is possible that, like the Greek god Hercules, Quetzacoatl was a man who raised himself to the level of a god through extraordinary efforts and achievements.

The Aztec legends tell that Quetzacoatl (whether he was a god or a man) was the philosopher-king of the Toltec people. Known as the god of wind, intellect, and transformation, Quetzacoatl incurred the wrath of many Toltec priests when he opposed the taking of human lives in sacrifice. Quetzacoatl believed in and practiced the art of self-mutilation; he pierced his tongue and earlobes regularly as a form of sacrifice. But he opposed the taking of lives.

When he was 52 years old (he was born in the year One Reed), Quetzacoatl was exiled from Tula. He went to the coast near where Veracruz stands today. There he lit a fire and burned himself. According to the Toltec and later the Mexica stories, he was lifted into the stars and became one of the shining lights of the universe. According to another legend, he sailed away to the East, promising to return.

Part of the legends and stories of Quetzacoatl was the belief that he would return one day to restore justice and harmony among the Mexican people. He would stop human sacrifices, and he would reign once more as the great philosopher-king.

son's inheritance. Malinali had been one of 20 women given by the tribal leaders of Potonchan to Cortés about a week earlier.

Geronimo de Aguilar was a Spaniard who had been shipwrecked on the Mayan coast about eight years earlier. He and a companion had survived the wreck and had lived with the Mayans ever since. When Cortés and the

Cortés and the Spaniards landed on this beach on the eastern coast of Mexico near Cempoallan in 1519. The Spaniards' beards, clothing, armor, and horses were unlike anything the Aztecs had ever seen before.

Spaniards arrived off the coast in March 1519, Aguilar rejoined his countrymen.

Hernán Cortés was a 34-year-old Spaniard. Rumors of the mysterious, rich kingdom of the Aztecs reached him in Cuba, where he had been living for the past 10 years.

It was April 22, 1519—Easter Sunday. Governor Tentlil approached the Spaniards with trepidation.

Although they looked like men, it was possible that they were gods. To Tentlil, the Spanish ships looked like huge floating mountains, and the Spaniard's armor and swords were unlike anything he had ever seen. Most disturbing were the horses, which looked like huge deer that the Spaniards could ride rapidly up and down the beach. These strangers and their creatures were indeed an amazing sight to behold.

In addition to this sight was the timing of their arrival. According to the Aztec calendar, the Spaniards had arrived at the beginning of the year *Ce Acatl* (One Reed). Like all Aztecs, Governor Tentlil knew that the god Quetzacoatl had been born in the year One Reed, had gone away into exile in another year One Reed (52 years later), and that the priests believed he would return in a One Reed year. Perhaps, Tentlil thought, he was the very first Aztec official to meet with the returned Quetzacoatl.

Tentlil knew it was necessary to extend the proper courtesy. Tentlil approached the strangers, was guided to the one who was their leader, and offered bits of his own blood on straws – the highest gesture of respect an Aztec leader could offer. Every Aztec knew that the world and the universe depended upon the exchange of blood between humans and the gods.

However, the strangers looked past the blood offering, at Tentlil himself, and began to ask questions in a rapid tongue. The governor had never heard such speech before, but he listened, and tried to understand.

Hand gestures can convey many things, but they can not express abstract ideas such as "the Aztec kingdom" or the substance of religious beliefs. Tentlil was frustrated by the difficulty of communication, as were the Spaniards. Then, the Spaniards brought forth Malinali. She understood both Nahautl, the Aztec language, and Mayan. After she heard what Tentlil had to say in Nahautl, she turned to Aguilar and spoke to him in Mayan. Aguilar then turned to Cortés and spoke in Spanish. Soon a four-way conversation was underway.

Tentlil knew the importance of courtesy and was disturbed when Cortés kept inquiring about Lord Montezuma, the Aztec emperor, whose name meant "He-who-shoots-flaming-arrows." After attempting to deflect the questions, Tentlil finally asked why Cortés wanted to know about the lord of the Aztec Empire.

Mainali told Tentlil that Cortés wanted to meet Lord Montezuma.

By now Tentlil had some doubts about the strangers. They were powerful and frightening men, but why would the god Quetzacoatl ask about Montezuma and where he was? Would not Quetzacoatl know the answer to such questions? Also, the repeated questions were a sign of rudeness. Tentlil mustered up his courage and told Malinali, who told Aguilar, who told Cortés, that many leaders of the Aztec Empire never had the good fortune to see Montezuma in their lives. It was absurd for an absolute stranger to appear and ask for what much more deserving people had yet to attain.

However, Cortés continued to ask to see Montezuma. When pressed for a reason, Cortés said he too was the servant of a great lord, King Charles, across the ocean. If they returned without having met Lord Montezuma, King Charles would be greatly displeased with them.

Perhaps it was at that moment that Tentlil decided the Spaniards were not gods. No god such as Quetzacoatl would declare that he was the representative of another. Perhaps they were only clever and powerful men.

Courtesy and diplomacy required that Tentlil leave before he became irritated with Cortés's boldness. He communicated through Malinali and Aguilar that he would send messages at once to Montezuma, telling him

Hernán Cortés owed much of his success as a leader to his charismatic personality, decisiveness, and diplomacy. As Tentlil discovered upon their first meeting, Cortés was also very persistent—he demanded to meet Montezuma, chief speaker of the Aztecs.

of the Spaniards' arrival. He would also have his artists draw pictures of them and their creatures now, so that the pictures might be sent to Montezuma. But as for seeing them in person, that would depend entirely upon Montezuma.

Before he departed, Tentlil placed 2,000 of his people at the disposal of the Spaniards. He ordered his men to build huts for them on the beach and to provide them with food. Then Tentlil prepared to withdraw.

Just before he could leave, the strangers put on a demonstration of their might. The horses pranced and thundered down the length of the beach, making huge indents in the sand. Even worse, the Spaniards put on a display with their guns, the likes of which had never been seen by the Indians. The Aztecs' only weapons were knives made of obsidian, or volcanic glass. Tentlil, who had begun to doubt whether the strangers were gods, now returned to his original thoughts. They came early in the year One Reed, they came from the direction of the rising sun, and they had great powers. Perhaps despite their uncouth ways, these were representatives of the great god Quetzacoatl.

One of the strangers, whose name was Bernal Diaz, later wrote his recollection about the end of the meeting in *The True History of the Conquest of Mexico*:

Tendile . . . remarked at this time a partly gilt helmet with one of our soldiers, and observed that it resembled one which had belonged to their ancestors, and which was placed on the head of their god Huitzilopochtli; he therefore expressed a wish to carry it to Montezuma. Cortés immediately presented it to him, saying at the same time, that in order to ascertain what resemblance existed between the gold of the two countries, it would not be amiss to return it filled with grains of that metal, as a fit present for our emperor. Tendile now took his leave, assuring Cortés that he would speedily return with the answer to his request. The intelligence of what had passed, together with our presents, was rapidly conveyed to Montezuma.

This was the first mention of gold. It would not be the last.

Two Worlds:
Aztec Mexico and
Christian Spain

Tenochtitlan was founded by the Aztecs around 1325 on an island on the west side of Lake Texcoco in the Valley of Mexico. This site would later become Mexico City, the capital of Mexico.

In that year [1432] the Tenochtitlan ruler Itzcoatzin was able to come out into the open, for he ruled everywhere, over rulers from town to town. Here, finally, began the glory of the Mexicatl Tenochtcatl, etc.

—The Codex Chimalpopoca

Governor Tentlil came from the tribe called Coahilua-Mexica. Today we call them the Aztecs. Hernán Cortés came from Spain by way of Cuba. Today we call him and his men the conquistadors.

The Aztec Empire encompassed much of Central America. It was built on the foundations of two or three earlier civilizations. There had been hundreds, even thousands of years of development which had led to the creation of the most evolved and sophisticated civilization seen in Central or North America.

The Aztecs were relative newcomers to the area. According to their tribal history, they migrated south from a place called Aztlan on the advice of their gods. The Aztecs had wandered for many years before settling on an island on the west side of Lake Texcoco in the Valley of Mexico. They called this island Tenochtitlan, and their histories indicate it was first settled around 1325.

For the first 100 years of their settlement, the Aztecs were only one of a number of tribes that vied for power and influence. Even as they gained military strength, the Aztecs remained in awe of the cultural and architectural accomplishments of those who had come before them. Just 20 miles away from Tenochtitlan, not far from the east bank of Lake Texcoco, stood the majestic ruins of the city of Teotihuacan, which means "The Place Where Men Became Gods." Terraces and ruined buildings surrounded an enormous pyramid, the Pyramid of the Sun, which rivaled Egyptian pyramids in size and appearance. Even after the Aztecs became the most powerful tribe in the region, leaders such as Lord Montezuma went to Teotihuacan once every 20 days to meditate and pray.

During the second 100 years of their occupation of Tenochtitlan, the Aztecs became the aggressors. They skillfully played older tribes against each other and made or unmade alliances as it suited them. All this time, the Aztecs were developing the most formidable military yet seen in Central America.

The Aztec army was designed to terrify, to overwhelm, but not to annihilate its foes. The Aztecs saw no point in destroying other peoples, who, if they survived, would make excellent subjects and payers of tribute. Therefore, the Aztecs took on their enemies, subjugated them, or enveloped them, but did not seek to wipe them out. Rather than force the defeated peoples to become part of the Aztec tribe, the Aztecs preferred to send officials, such as Tentlil, to govern them and to supervise the collection of tributes. Otherwise, however, the Aztecs remained very much to themselves, the "ruling people" of the Valley of Mexico.

Success followed success during the 15th century. The Aztecs expanded from Tenochtitlan and conquered many of their enemies. They surrounded others and hoped that the enemy cities would eventually fall to them through a natural process of envelopment. This was the strategy used with one of their neighbors to the east, the Tlaxcallan tribe. As the empire continued to grow, the Aztecs demanded vast amounts of tribute from their subject peoples. One historian gives the following example of the types of tributes the Aztecs collected:

> Twenty chests of ground chocolate; 40 pieces of armour, of a particular device; 2,400 loads of large mantles, or woven cloth; 800 loads of small mantles, of rich wearing apparel; 5 pieces of armour, of rich feathers; 60 pieces of armour, of common feathers; a chest of beans; a chest of china; a chest of maize; 8,000 reams of paper; likewise 2,000 loaves of very white salt, refined in the shape of a mould, for the consumption only of the lords of Mexico.

Chocolate, cloth, and feathers were important, but the most important tribute came in the form of human beings. As they conquered, the Aztecs came more and more to see blood and human sacrifice as essential. Since they were a warrior people, the Aztecs venerated the war god Huitzliopochtli above all others. According to the Aztec religion, Huitzliopochtli fought for the preservation of the world and the universe against the powers of destruction. To placate Huitzliopochtli and keep him active in the fight for survival, the Aztecs made larger and larger numbers of human sacrifices.

Sacrifices were conducted by Aztec priests. Throughout the empire, but most especially atop the Great Temple in Tenochtitlan, priests cut out the hearts of living prisoners with obsidian knives and presented the still-beating hearts as offerings to Huitzliopochtli. The ritual grew in size and number so that by the start of the 16th century, there may well have been as many as 10,000 people sacrificed each year throughout the Aztec Empire.

People today see this ritual as barbaric and preposterous. It is important to remember, however, that many cultures and civilizations have practiced human sacrifice. It is the enormous number of human sacrifices made by the Aztecs that distinguishes them from other practitioners of this ritual. The Aztecs firmly believed that only through blood offerings to the gods could they hope to avoid the obliteration of the world and themselves.

Montezuma took the Aztec throne in 1502. He was then about 30 years old and was known as a mystical man, devoted to the cult of Huitzliopochtli. Soon after becoming the Aztec leader (his actual title was *tlatoani,* which means "chief speaker"), Montezuma led his warriors on several ambitious campaigns. It was necessary to do this early in his reign to establish himself as a sound military leader. That completed, he settled down to a majestic life as the spiritual and political leader of the Aztec Empire. He lived in regal splendor in Tenochtitlan. Montezuma could sample food from as many as 100 dishes at a meal, and he seldom wore the same clothing twice. Much of this

Aztec priests performed human sacrifices atop the Great Temple in Tenochtitlan. This gruesome ritual was thought to placate the war god Huitzliopochtli and keep the Aztec Empire strong.

wealth came from the tribute he and his predecessors imposed on the conquered peoples.

In 1507, the Aztecs performed a New Fire ceremony, the most important in their religion. The Aztec calendar operated on a 52-year cycle, starting with the year One Rabbit and ending with the year One Rabbit. The Aztecs viewed the end of their cycle in much the same way that Christians viewed the end of a century or even a millennium. When the day came, the Aztecs extinguished all fires in their city and in the Valley of Mexico for five days and nights. Utensils and items were thrown out to prepare for a new beginning. After five solemn days of darkness and quiet, the Aztec priests announced the beginning of a new 52-year cycle. The world had been reborn; the gods were satisfied with the sacrifices of their chosen people.

The new cycle that commenced in 1507 was interrupted by the appearance of the Spanish strangers in the year One Reed (1519). Two cultures and two worlds met and clashed.

Spain had only been unified in 1492. Throughout the late Middle Ages, Spain had been split into several parts: Castile, which was Christian; Aragon, which was Christian; and Granada, which was Muslim. Two things worked to bring Spain together: a marriage and a conquest.

Ferdinand of Aragon married Isabela of Castile in 1469. Though they continued to rule their two domains separately, the king and queen were working toward unification. In January 1492, the last Moorish king of Granada surrendered his city and land to Ferdinand and Isabela, thereby ending the 700-year Spanish *Reconquista* ("Reconquest").

The wealth they obtained from the surrender of Granada enabled Ferdinand and Isabela to sponsor an Italian sailor named Columbus. He sailed from Spain

Spain was reunited in 1492 with the defeat of the last Moorish king of Granada. Ferdinand of Aragon and Isabela of Castile, depicted here, started this reunification with their marriage in 1469.

in August 1492 and landed on an island in the Bahamas on October 12 (which island it was remains open to dispute). Through this voyage and the three others later undertaken, Columbus opened the way for the newly unified Spain to exert its will in the New World (Western Hemisphere).

A whole generation of Spaniards grew up hearing stories about brave Columbus and the noble King Ferdinand and Queen Isabela. Since there were no longer any Moors or Arabs in Spain to fight, adventurous young men began to look west as a way to earn their knightly spurs and, perhaps, to find gold. One of these young men was Hernán Cortés.

Born in Medellin, a town in southern Castile, Cortés grew up the son of an impoverished *hidalgo* (Spanish knight). Some of his friends and a biographer claim he was a sickly child and that his life was despaired of several times, but as an adult Cortés would be vigorous, head-strong, and above all, daring.

From Columbus's first discoveries in the Bahamas and in the central Caribbean, other Spanish explorers had struck off in different directions. Hispaniola, which today comprises the two nations of Haiti and the Dominican Republic, was one of the first significant areas of settlement; a second area was the island of Cuba, which is where Hernán Cortés went in the year 1506.

From the beginning, Spanish colonists exhibited an almost overwhelming desire to find gold. What gold existed on Hispaniola and Cuba was brought to them by Indians within the first 20 years of settlement, and ambitious young men such as Hernán Cortés began to think about seeking gold in other areas to the west.

The governor of Cuba, Diego Velasquez, had similar ambitions. In 1517 and 1518, he sent expeditions to the mainland, which had not been well explored. Hernández de Cordova landed on the Yucatan peninsula and made his way partway along the coast, but returned to Cuba without finding any gold. Juan de Grijalva also started his expedition along the Yucatan coast and he made his way further north, reaching the area of present-day Veracruz. It was this expedition that alerted the Aztec leaders to the arrival of strangers. Grijalva also, however, returned to his ships and sailed away. His appearance had given a shock to the Aztec leaders, but months passed without anything untoward happening, so Montezuma and the Aztecs tried to forget about the appearance of the strangers.

In the autumn of 1518, Governor Velasquez searched for a man suitable to lead a third Spanish expedition.

There were plenty of willing and able men, but Velasquez settled on Cortés. In October, the adventurous Spaniard was named commander of the new expedition. The commission dated October 23, 1518, authorized Cortés to probe the coast of the mainland and to find gold where possible. But the actual work of finding the men to go was up to Cortés.

Cortés was a man who had done much in his life, but had so far achieved rather little. His had not been a brilliant career, but this opportunity brought out something in him. At the very beginning it called on his abilities to promote. Cortés had a splendid flag made, embroidered with the words: "Brothers and Comrades, in true faith let us follow the Holy Cross and we shall conquer." It did not matter that Cortés was less than devout or that his recruits were also worldly men. The banner was a splendid success, and by late winter Cortés had recruited about 600 men for the venture west.

Bernal Diaz, one of his soldiers, provided a description of Cortés:

> He was of good stature and strong build, of a rather pale complexion, and serious countenance. His features were, if faulty, rather too small; his eyes mild and grace. His beard was black, thick, and scanty; his hair in the same manner. His breast and shoulders were broad, and his body very thin. He was very well limbed, and his legs rather bowed; an excellent horseman, and dexterous in the use of arms.

Just before Cortés and his men were ready to depart, Governor Velasquez regretted choosing Cortez as commander. Velasquez tried to stop Cortés, whom he now saw as too ambitious and headstrong, but it was too late. Cortés and his men sailed from Cuba in mid-February 1519.

Malinali acted as Cortés's translator and counselor. She is pictured here standing to Cortés's left as they meet the Aztecs for the first time.

Cortés landed in early April at the town of Potonchan, near the border between present-day Mexico and Guatemala. After a fierce battle with the Indians there, Cortés met with their chiefs and made peace. As a gesture of friendship, the chiefs gave them 20 Indian women, who could make tortillas for the Spaniards. One of these was Malinali. The Spaniards baptized her with the name "Dona Marina."

Malinali was the single most important tool Cortés obtained. Without her to translate, Cortés would have been unable to communicate with the Aztecs or other

Malinali—Dona Marina— Malinche

Malinali's tale is remarkable and tragic. Some see her as a terrible traitor, while others consider her the Mother of Mexico.

Malinali, which means "sharp blade of grass," was a teenager when the chiefs of Potonchan gave her to the Spaniards in 1519. She had been born to a noble Mayan family, but her mother and stepfather sold her into slavery so she would not pose any threat to the inheritance of her younger half-brother. By the time she was given to the Spaniards, Malinali was a confirmed survivor, someone who would make the best of a bad situation.

The Indian girl proved her worth to the Spanish conquistadors during the conversation between Tentlil, Cortés, and Aguilar. Soon she was known as "Dona Marina," an important member of the Spanish expedition.

Malinali and Cortés became lovers sometime that year, and she became his chief counselor as well as his interpreter. When Cortés and Montezuma met on the causeway to Tenochtitlan, Malinali stood right beside him, and, along with Aguilar, translated from Nahautl to Mayan, and Mayan to Spanish.

Her birth name was Malinali; the Spaniards called her "Dona Marina"; and the Aztecs called her "Malinche," which later became a synonym for a traitor to one's people.

Indians. Just as important, she became his chief counselor, advising him about the practices and culture of the Aztecs and others.

We have already seen how Cortés landed on the beach at Chalchiuhcuecan and began his interaction with the Totonac natives. The first exchanges were full of questions for both sides. Governor Tentlil hoped the Spanish would pick up and leave, as two other groups of Spaniards had done in 1517 and 1518. Cortés wanted to see Lord Montezuma, and to find more of the gold and silver that it was rumored the Aztecs possessed.

Cortés built Villa Rica de la Vera Cruz in 1519, and had himself elected governor. As governor, he could grant himself a commission to continue his adventures in Mexico, and circumvent the restrictions placed on him by Governor Velasquez of Cuba.

Parry and Thrust: The Spanish Advance on Tenochtitlan

Gentlemen, our fame will exceed far that of the most illustrious of our predecessors, who never, as you observe, dared to take such a measure; and therefore it is better, instead of repining, to look forward, and leave all to be guided by the hand of God.

—Cortés speaking to his men about his having scuttled their ships, quoted by Bernal Diaz, in *The True History of the Conquest of Mexico*

From his first meeting with Governor Tentlil, Hernán Cortés insisted that he must see Montezuma. To do any less would bring down the wrath of his lord, King Charles.

Tentlil brought communications from Montezuma within a matter of days. The Aztec leader was pleased that the strangers had come to his land, and he even hoped that others would come at another time. Montezuma had been pleased to fill the helmet with gold dust, although the Aztecs did not understand the fascination it held for the strangers. (The Aztecs preferred jade and turquoise.) But it was impossible for Montezuma to meet with them; he was occupied in Tenochtitlan and could not go to the ocean. As for the strangers, they could not go to Tenochtitlan; the way was hindered by deserts and rough terrain. Unfortunately for the Aztecs, Montezuma's message was contradicted by the fact that Tentlil's runners had been able to make it to Tenochtitlan and back within one week.

Cortés continued to insist that he meet Montezuma. But for the moment, the Spanish leader had other concerns. Many of his men were grumbling that the expedition had become too hazardous, that they had done well to obtain the gifts given to them by Tentlil, and that it was time to return to Cuba. That was the last thought in Cortés's mind. He knew that if he returned to Cuba without having achieved great things, he would be imprisoned by Governor Velasquez. By sailing without Velasquez' permission, Cortés had made himself an outlaw. Therefore, Cortés did two bold things.

First, he created the first Spanish town on the mainland of Central America. Named Villa Rica de la Vera Cruz, it was just a garrison outpost, a fort with wooden walls, at first. By establishing the municipality, Cortés could have himself elected as its governor. Then he could proceed to grant himself a commission to do anything that had been denied him in the commission granted by Governor Velasquez. It was a clever piece of legal fiction, but it worked. Soon Cortés had a legal basis for continuing his adventures.

The new town was founded on June 28, 1519. By an odd

Charles V, Holy Roman Emperor, supported Cortés's exploration of Mexico. Cortés ensured Charles's continued support by honoring the "king's fifth" — a Spanish law that mandated that one-fifth of all treasures discovered overseas be sent to the king.

coincidence, Charles I, King of Spain, was elected Charles the V, Holy Roman Emperor that same day. Even though Cortés was not aware of this elevation, it made Charles the monarch with the most land in Christendom.

Second, Cortés had his 11 ships destroyed. This was risky, even foolhardy. Cortés wanted to make sure there was no way to escape. He wanted to force his men to be with him in any and all situations. He accomplished this by sinking the ships in which they had sailed from Cuba. The "floating mountains" that had so impressed the Indians were no more.

Emperor Charles V

History records few leaders like Charles V. He rose to hold more land and titles than any other European monarch, yet he chose to abdicate and retire to a monastery. Though he shared the stage with other great leaders of the era, such as King Henry VIII of England and King Francis I of France, Charles V may well have been the most remarkable European leader of his time.

Born in Ghent, Belgium, in 1500, Charles was the grandson of Ferdinand and Isabela, the king and queen of Spain, on his mother's side and Maximilian, the Holy Roman Emperor, on his father's. He became king of Spain in 1516, and Holy Roman Emperor in 1519. He commissioned Ferdinand Magellan to sail around the world (the first circumnavigation), and it was in his name that Hernán Cortés conquered Mexico and Francisco Pizarro conquered Peru. By 1540 Charles led an empire that encompassed numerous parts of Europe and a significant part of Central and South America. He was the most powerful and richest monarch of his day.

The great thorn in his side was the Protestant religion, begun by Martin Luther in 1517. Luther's followers came to dominate northern Germany, and Emperor Charles spent years of his time and millions of his ducats in fruitless efforts to subdue the Protestants, whom he considered heretics.

Charles's nobility often shone through in difficult circumstances. Shortly after Martin Luther's peaceful death, the emperor and his followers stood near Luther's grave. Many urged the emperor to exhume the body and display it. Charles demurred, saying, "I do not make war on dead men."

Years of war and of travel wore Charles out. In 1556 he officially abdicated all his titles and powers in an extraordinary ceremony in Belgium. To his son Philip he gave the Spanish crown and the New World possessions; to his younger brother Ferdinand, Charles gave Austria and the title of Holy Roman Emperor. The division between the Spanish Habsburgs (started by Philip) and the Austrian Habsburgs (started by Ferdinand) began that day.

Charles retired to a monastery at Yuste, Spain. Although he lived more comfortably than his fellow monks, he was one of them until his death two years later in 1558. Europe had not seen Charles's like since Charlemagne, and she would not see another like him until Napoleon Bonaparte.

By July it was clear that Cortés intended to move inland, to see the great city of Tenochtitlan. Some of his men may still have been against the idea, but they had no choice. Their captain had deprived them of choices by scuttling the ships.

Cortés had learned much in the three months he had been on the coast. Loyal Aztecs such as Tentlil had tried to persuade him that the Aztec Empire was too mighty to confront, but Cortés had visited other towns like Cempoallan. There he had learned that many of the Totonac people whom Tentlil governed were discontent, and that many people throughout Mexico resented the vast amounts of tribute forced from them. Seeing the discontent that existed, Cortés believed he could find a way to drive an even stronger wedge between the Aztec and their subject peoples. On July 30, Cortés left the coast with about 350 Spaniards, and about 2,000 Totonac people who acted as porters and allies. The invasion of Mexico had begun.

Montezuma was informed of every change, however slight, in the activities and movements of the Spaniards. Back in Tenochtlitlan, Montezuma was urged by his younger brother, Cuithauac, and his cousin, Catahomec, to strike at the invaders before they could reach the Valley of Mexico. There were plenty of spots for ambush on the road the Spaniards took. So the question remains: why did Montezuma not order an attack?

Traditionally, the answer given is that Montezuma believed the Spaniards to be gods and that he could not harm them. However, there was at least one other more practical reason for Montezuma's failure to attack: The Aztec armies mobilized and fought only during the dry season, which began in November and ran through early spring. The wet season, when Cortés arrived, was not a time for military action. Thus, both the idea that the Spaniards might be gods and traditional Aztec military behavior limited Montezuma's choices. He stayed his hand and the Spaniards continued to approach.

The distance Cortez and his men traveled from Veracruz to Mexico City is less than 200 miles, but it is an uphill road which climbs to 7,000 feet above sea level. By the time they reached the land of the Tlaxcallan peoples, the Spaniards were foot sore and bone weary.

Tlaxcalla was a semiautonomous nation located slightly to the east of the Valley of Mexico. The Tlaxcallans had fought the Aztecs for nearly two generations and had managed to avoid being swallowed up by them. In these circumstances, the Aztecs had decided long ago to leave Tlaxcalla alone, to allow them to slowly wither and die, rather than try to conquer them outright. This was in accordance with the Aztec military strategy, which had succeeded against many of their prior enemies. But it left an island of Aztec-haters along the route of the Spaniards under Cortés.

Although the Tlaxcallan people hated the Aztecs, they did not like the appearance of the Spaniards either. Unlike the Totonacs of the coast who had made an alliance with Cortés, the Tlaxcallans were determined to resist him. Bernal Diaz, the Spanish infantrymen, later recalled the battle:

> These troops were all clad and bore devices of white and red, which was the uniform of their general. Those who were armed with lances closed upon us while we were embarrassed in the broken ground, but as soon as we arrived on the plain with our cavalry and artillery, we made them smart for it. Notwithstanding this they closed upon us on every side, insomuch that we could not venture to move, and we were in the greatest danger but that the hand of God assisted us.

When the fighting took place on broken ground or in the woods, the Tlaxcallans prevailed, but when it was brought onto an open field or plain, the Spaniards had the advantage. Diaz commented, "The loss of the enemy on this occasion was very considerable, eight of their principal chiefs being amongst the number. As soon as we found ourselves clear of them we returned thanks to God for his mercy, and entering a strong and spacious temple, we dressed our wounds with the fat of Indians. Of 15 wounded men, only one died."

The Tlaxcallans did not give up the fight immediately. Their general and leader remained adamantly opposed to the Spaniards and would have led his men to fight to the bitter end. But other members of the Tlaxcallan leadership thought differently. Even if they were to overcome the Spanish, it would be a Pyrrhic victory (a victory at too great a cost, named for the Greek General Pyrrhus). The Tlaxcallans would emerge from such a battle so exhausted that they would be easy prey for the Aztecs in the future. Therefore, the top members of the Tlaxcallan tribe decided to negotiate with the Spaniards. On September 25, Cortés and his men entered the chief Tlaxcallan city.

Negotiations were delicate because Cortés insisted on forcing his Christian views on the Tlaxcallans. From the very beginning of his adventure, Cortés had seen his actions as double in meaning and importance. First, he wanted to subdue the Aztecs and all the other Indians of Mexico to his will and the rule of Charles V. Second, Cortés wanted the Indians to embrace Christianity.

There had been some early successes in Cortés's attempts to convert the Indians. The Mayan Indians of Yucatan had happily added the Virgin Mary to their list of deities, and for years after the meeting with Cortés Mayan canoes greeted Spanish ships with cries of "Maria! Maria!" and "Cortés! Cortés!"

Now however, Cortés was in the heart of Mexican country. The Tlaxcallans did not understand, and they

ycmon avatecque .tlaxcalla.

Cortés and the Spaniards were determined to bring Christianity to the Indians of Mexico. However, the Indians only superficially accepted Christianity by adding figures like the Virgin Mary to their pantheon.

bitterly resented Cortés's desire to force Christianity upon them. The most they would consent to was that one of the several temples in their major city be cleansed of idols; Cortés was allowed to place statues of the Virgin Mary there. With this concession won, Cortés returned to his other main point: conquest.

Given that the Tlaxcallans had fought so long and hard against the Aztecs, they were quite willing to serve with Cortés in a campaign against them. When he departed from the Tlaxcallan city on October 10, he had over 5,000 Tlaxcallan allies with him.

Cortés decided not to take the advice of the Tlaxcallan leaders, who urged a direct march on Tenochtitlan. Instead,

Cortés, the Spaniards, and their Indian allies went by way of Chollan, which was a major Aztec city dedicated to the worship of the god Quetzacoatl. This route brought Cortés and the members of his expedition into great danger. Once they were inside the walls of Chollan, the Spaniards could be surrounded at any moment without hope of escape.

Knowing this, Cortés insisted his men sleep in their armor with their weapons directly at their sides. When the surprise attack did come on the morning of October 15, the Spaniards were more than ready. Using their swords and blades made of Toledo steel, the Spaniards won a convincing battle in the courtyard of Chollan. Hundreds of the people were killed; very few Spaniards suffered more than slight wounds. The result of the victory was to enhance the idea that the Spaniards were invulnerable. Hearing the news in Tenochtitlan, the Lord Montezuma fell into a deep despair.

The months since the Spaniards landed had been debilitating for Montezuma. He alternated between self-pity, fury at the gods, and outright despair. Believing that his destiny had come, Montezuma had a large statue carved of himself in the area of Chapultpec, on the mainland just outside of the city of Tenochtitlan. This was seen by many of his nobles as a gesture of surrender. Aztec kings tended to have their carving made when they believed death was imminent.

There were still some who urged Montezuma to make a stand. His brother and cousin disdained the idea that the Spaniards were gods and insisted they were nothing more than vicious marauders and pirates. Let the Aztec army be summoned! Let the invaders be destroyed!

The entreaties of his kinsmen were to no avail. Montezuma awaited the arrival of the strangers, as if his doom had already been written in the stars.

Tenochtitlan's impressive temples, stone buildings, and wooden causeways showcased the advances of Aztec architecture and engineering. Cortés and the Spaniards were impressed with the city's beauty, as well as the thousands of Aztecs who greeted them upon their arrival.

The Eighth of November: Montezuma and Cortés Meet in Tenochtitlan

Is it true that you are the King Motechzoma?

—Miguel Leon-Portilla, *The Broken Spears*

On November 8, Cortés, the Spaniards, and their allies came into the Valley of Mexico and approached the causeway that led to Tenochtitlan from the south. By now the Spaniards had already had a good look from a distance of one of the most impressive sights they had ever seen.

Cortés and his men, Bernal Diaz among them, gazed long and softly on the spectacle beneath them. Though they were men of the world, most of the Spaniards had never seen a sight to equal what was spread before them on and around the lake.

Stone buildings were intermingled with wooden causeways.

Floating gardens, called *chinampas,* displayed the bounteous Aztec agriculture. Temples reared up throughout the city but were most noticeable in the central part. And people— thousands upon thousands of them—were gazing up at the Spaniards and their Indian allies.

In all his travels, Christopher Columbus had never seen such a sight; neither had Balboa or other Spanish explorers. November 8, 1519 marked the moment when two worlds, developed in isolation from each other, truly met.

It was a moment that might well have produced fear on both sides, but Hernán Cortés approached Tenochititlan without trepidation. Born in the Spain of Columbus and reared on stories of Spanish knights, he moved like one who knew his destiny had arrived. Rather than display any hesitation, Cortés gave the order and led his mixed group of Spaniards and Indians down the slopes toward the lake and city.

Bernal Diaz described the situation:

On the next day we set out, accompanied as on the former one, and proceeded by the grand causeway, which is eight yards wide, and runs in a straight line to the city of Mexico. It was crowded with people, as were all the towers, temples, and causeways, in every part of the lake, attracted by curiosity to behold men, and animals, such as never had been before seen in these countries. We were occupied by very different thoughts; our number did not amount to 450, we had perfectly in our recollection the accounts we had received on our march, that we were to be put to death on our arrival in the city, which we now saw before us, approachable only by causeways, whereon were several bridges, the breaking of one of which effectually cut off our retreat. And now let who can, tell me, where are men in this world to be found except ourselves, who would have hazarded such an attempt?

Roughly one year later, Cortés recalled the scene in a letter to Emperor Charles V:

> After we had crossed this bridge, Mutezuma came to greet us and with him some two hundred lords, all barefoot and dressed in a different costume, but also very rich in their way and more so than the others. They came in two columns, pressed very close to the walls of the street, which is very wide and beautiful and so straight that you can see from one end to the other. It is two-thirds of a league long and has on both sides very good and big houses, both dwellings and temples . . . Mutezuma came down the middle of this street with two chiefs, one on his right hand and the other on his left. One of these was that great chief who had come on a litter to speak with me, and the other was Mutezuma's brother, chief of the city of Yztapalapa, which I had left that day. And they were all dressed alike except that Mutezuma wore sandals whereas the others went barefoot; and they held his arm on either side. When we met I dismounted and stepped forward to embrace him, but the two lords who were with him stopped me with their hands so that I should not touch him; and they likewise all performed the ceremony of kissing the earth. When this was over Mutezuma requested his brother to remain with me and to take me by the arm while he went a little way ahead with the other; and after he had spoken to me all the others in the two columns came and spoke with me, one after another, and then each returned to his column.

The meeting was friendly but full of portent. Both leaders and both groups of men sized each other up that afternoon.

The Aztec Dynasty

We call Montezuma the Aztec emperor, but a literal translation of the title *tlatoani* is closer to "chief speaker." The title came from early Aztec history when each section of the Aztec tribe elected its own "speaker." These men then elected a "chief speaker," who governed with considerable but not unchecked power.

The following is a list of the chief speakers, the meanings of their names, and the dates they ruled the Aztecs:

Acamapichtli	[Reed-fist]	1372-1391
Huitzilihuitl	[Hummingbird-feather]	1391-1417
Chimalpopoca	[He-smokes-like-a-shield]	1417-1427
Itzacoatl	[Obsidian-serpent]	1427-1440
Moteuczoma Ilhuicamina	[He-who-shoots-flaming-arrows]	1440-1468
Axayacatl	[Water-mask]	1468-1486
Ahuitzotl	[Water-porcupine]	1486-1502
Moteuczoma Xoxoyotl	[He-who-shoots-flaming-arrows the-younger]	1502-1520
Cuitlahua	[Excrement-owner]	1520-1520
Cuauhtemoc	[He-descends-like-an-eagle]	1520-1525

When Montezuma the Younger took the throne in 1502, the post of chief speaker was more like an emperor than had previously been the case. Montezuma enhanced the dignity of his office, as well, by demanding that no one look him in the face. As a result, his nobles were deeply offended when Cortés and other Spaniards did so. Montezuma, who was the priest of the god Huitzliopochtli even before he became the chief speaker, also increased the number of sacrifices to the war god.

However, the absolute power Montezuma exercised over his subjects became a problem. When the Spaniards first arrived, Montezuma was uncertain how to proceed against them. Many of the high Aztec nobles wished to strike against the invaders, but were prevented from doing so; they could not violate the wishes of the chief speaker.

The first meeting between Cortés and Montezuma was friendly. Malinali and Aguilar translated the conversation between the leaders. It would be the first of many meetings that would take place over the following weeks.

Cortés and Montezuma were both leaders, but they were about as different as two men could be. The latter had spent his entire life in a sort of royal cocoon, calm and sure that events would unfold in his favor. The former had been a lackluster adventurer just one year ago; now he was the leader of a band of desperate men. The age difference, too, showed. Cortés was in his early thirties; Montezuma was about a decade older. Very likely Cortés assessed Montezuma as an older man without the stomach for a major fight. For his part, Montezuma believed that this was the god Quetzacoatl, come to reclaim his throne and dominion in Mexico. An Aztec record of the meeting reflects this belief:

> When Motecuhzoma had given necklaces to each one, Cortés asked him: "Are you Motecuhzoma? Are you the king? Is it true that you are the King Motecuhzoma?"
>
> And the king said: "Yes, I am Motecuhzoma." Then he stood up to welcome Cortés; he came forward, bowed his head low and addressed him in these words: "Our lord, you are weary. The journey has tired you, but now you have arrived on the earth. You have come to your city, Mexico. You have come here to sit on your throne, to sit under its canopy.
>
> "The kings who have gone before, your representatives, guarded it and preserved it for your coming. The Kings Itzcoatl, Motecuhzoma the Elder, Axaycatl, Tizoc and Ahuitzol ruled for you in the city of Mexico. The people were protected by their swords and sheltered by their shields
>
> "Do the kings know the destiny of those they left behind, their posterity? If only they are watching! If only they can see what I see!'
>
> "No, it is not a dream. I am not walking in my sleep. I am not seeing you in my dreams . . . I have seen you at last! I have met you face to face! I was in agony, for 10 days with my eyes fixed on the Region of the Mystery. And now you have come out of the clouds and mists to sit on your throne again.
>
> "This was foretold by the kings who governed your city, and now it has taken place. You have come back to us, you have come down from the sky. Rest now, and take possession of your royal houses. Welcome to your lands, my lords!"

The conversations between Cortés and Montezuma were translated by Malinali and Aguilar. Malinali may well have been frightened at meeting Montezuma—throughout her life his had been the presence that lay over Mexico, and she had learned early in life that he was the human incarnation of the god Huitzliopochtli. If she was terrified, Malinali kept her secret well.

Cortés replied that he came as a friend and that Montezuma should have no fear. Whether Montezuma took this as truth is impossible to say. When the first meeting ended, Cortés and the Spaniards were escorted to the palace.

Cortés and Montezuma met daily over the next week. We do not know the exact day, but we are certain from nearly all accounts that Montezuma took Cortés and a handful of the Spaniards up the steps of the Grand Temple in the very center of Tenochtitlan. This was the heart and soul of the Aztec Empire, the place where thousands of people had been sacrificed and from which Aztec warriors had sallied forth to conquer large sections of Mexico.

The massacre of the Aztecs at the hands of Pedro de Alvardo and the Spaniards was one of the bloodiest in Tenochtitlan's history. Alvardo attacked during an Aztec festival, and thousands of Aztec nobles and warriors were killed.

Uneasy Coexistence

When the dance was loveliest and when song was linked to song, the Spaniards were seized with an urge to kill the celebrants.

—Miguel Leon-Portilla, *The Broken Spears*

On November 14, 1519, just six days after he entered Tenochtitlan, Cortés made Montezuma his prisoner in the Spanish quarters. It was done deftly, with style and deception. In *Letters from Mexico,* Cortés writes to Emperor Charles V:

Most Invincible Lord, six days having passed since we first entered this great city of Temixitan, during which time I had seen something of it, though little compared with how much there is to see and record, I decided from what I had seen that it would benefit Your Royal service and our safety if Mutezuma were in my power and not in complete liberty, in order that he should not retreat from the willingness he showed to serve Your Majesty; but chiefly because we Spaniards are rather obstinate and persistent, and should we annoy him he might, as he is so powerful, obliterate all memory of us. Furthermore, by having him with me, all those other lands which were subject to him would come more swiftly to the recognition and service of Your Majesty, as later happened. I resolved, therefore, to take him and keep him in the quarters where I was, which were very strong.

Cortés and a group of his men went to Montezuma's palace. Cortés did most of the speaking with Malinali doing rapid translations. Cortés told Montezuma that he knew Montezuma had ordered some of his warriors to attack the Spanish fort at Veracruz. Montezuma denied this vehemently, but Cortés continued in an elegant combination of coercion and flattery. Assuring Montezuma that the emperor's well-being and safety were his chief concern, Cortés suggested that Montezuma move temporarily into the Spanish quarters as his guest. Of course, the argument ran that Montezuma was still the emperor and could give what orders he liked to his many subjects, but he would be safer and happier under Spanish protection.

From the first news he had received of the Spanish landing on the coast, Montezuma had shown he was unable to make firm and clear decisions. As his brother and cousin had said many times, there had been numerous opportunities to ambush the Spaniards on their way to Tenochtitlan. Now the Spaniards were within the city, and even worse, Montezuma agreed to go to the Spanish quarters as their honored guest.

Of all the many mistakes and miscalculations that Montezuma made, this one was probably the worst. He became a hostage held by Cortés.

The first days and weeks of captivity were not unpleasant for Montezuma. He gave orders that were passed out of the palace to his subordinates, and it appeared as if the chief speaker were still in command of his city. Bernal Diaz related some of the details of the emperor's captivity:

> In the morning, having paid his devotions, he eat a slight breakfast, not of meats but vegetables, such as agi or pepper, and then remained a full hour hearing business, in the manner I have already described. The number of judges and counsellors who attended upon him at those times amounted to twenty. His numerous mistresses he used to marry to his officers and particular friends; some of them fell to our lot; mine was called Donna Francisca; a lady of high birth, as she shewed by her manners. Thus sometimes amusing himself, and sometimes meditating on his situation, the great Montezuma passed the days of his confinement amongst us.

As Montezuma's kinsmen had warned, there was no limit to the greed and desire of the Spaniards. Soon after Montezuma was settled within his headquarters, Cortés began to ask that a large amount of silver and gold be compiled. Montezuma complied and the collection of valuables began forthwith.

However, events suddenly turned against Cortés. He received news of a new foe. This new foe was not the Aztecs, Tlaxcallans, or any other Indian group, but a large force of Spaniards sent from Cuba to arrest him as a traitor.

Bernal Diaz

Bernal Diaz was born in Medina del Campo, Spain, in 1496. He left Spain in 1514 and served on all three major Spanish expeditions to the mainland: with Cordoba in 1517, with Grijalva in 1518, and with Cortés in 1519. Diaz then served under Cortés and Alvarado in the invasion of Guatemala, in 1524.

He returned once or twice to Spain, but only for brief periods. Diaz settled in Guatemala, where he became a justice of the peace and leader of a hacienda. Late in life, he became incensed upon reading *Cortés: The Life of the Conqueror by his Secretary, Francisco Lopez de Gomara.* Diaz was upset that the tone of Gomara's book suggested that Cortés orchestrated and conducted the invasion of Mexico all on his own. Diaz sat down and took the next four years to write *The True History of the Conquest of Mexico*, which was published after his death.

Diaz was a wonderful narrator. He was an actual conquistador, one who became comfortable but not rich, and one who seemed to remember all the details of those fateful years from 1519 to 1521.

The True History of the Conquest of Mexico emphasizes time and again that Cortés was only the most skillful and adroit of a larger group, who collectively defeated the Aztecs. Whether or not Diaz presents an unbiased account of Cortés is difficult to determine, but he does balance much of the self-serving praise that Cortés heaps upon himself in his letters to Emperor Charles V.

Diaz died in Guatemala at the ripe age of 82. He was apparently the longest-lived of the conquistadors, and his book makes him perhaps the most memorable of a daring band of men.

Pánfilo Narváez had arrived on the coast of Mexico with about 900 men in arms.

Governor Diego Velasquez had not forgotten that Cortés had sailed against his orders. When Cortés left Cuba in February 1519, he did so as an outlaw, a man who had broken his agreement with the governor. For this reason, Cortés had created Villa Rica de la Vera Cruz as the first municipality on the mainland, so that the townspeople could vote him as their captain-general. Cortés had also taken the precaution of sending the "king's fifth" to Charles V. Spanish law dictated that one-fifth of all the gold and jewels found overseas must be returned to the king. Cortés had sent these as a way of creating a relationship with the king, independent of his relationship with Governor Velasquez.

Suddenly all of Cortés's earlier successes were at risk. He might have to yield his tenuous position in Tenochtitlan to fight Narváez—fighting fellow Spaniards to the east as he retreated from angry Aztecs in the west.

As was typical of Cortés, he made a quick decision. He announced to his men that he would take 400 of them and leave for the coast at once. He would leave a skeleton garrison of 80 to 120 men in Tenochtitlan under the command of Pedro de Alvarado. Cortés knew that Alvarado was an impetuous and willful man, but he also knew that the garrison there would fight to the death under his leadership. It was a bold gamble, worthy of the best traditions of Spanish knighthood.

Cortés departed from Tenochtitlan early in May 1520. Because he already had men out in the field, he left that day with only about 80 Spaniards, most of whom were clothed in the cotton armor they had been given by the Totonac Indians a year earlier. It seemed a pitiful force with which to oppose to Narváez. Cortés ensured his position in Tenochtitlan as well. Knowing that Alvarado was a high-strung, volatile man, Cortés made sure that each man of the Spanish garrison swore on a missal (Mass-book) to obey their new commander. With things as well settled as could be, Cortés left for the coast.

By then Narváez and his men had landed and marched to the Totonac village of Cempoallan. Narváez had also sent messengers to Villa Rica de la Vera Cruz, demanding the surrender of that town. The messengers had been taken prisoner and sent to Cortés, who, with his usual charm and generosity, had won them over to his side. Even so, Cortés marched with slightly over 200 Spaniards against Narváez's 900.

A short battle took place at Cempollan on May 26. Cortés made a surprise attack. With the loss of only four of his men, Cortés defeated the enemy. Narváez was badly wounded; he lost one of his eyes. Narváez became Cortés's prisoner, and the next day Cortés gained the loyalty of his former enemies. Bernal Diaz described the remarkable scene:

> By this time it was clear day. Cortés, seated in an arm chair, a mantle of orange colour thrown over his shoulders, his arms by his side, and surrounded by his officers and soldiers, received the salutations of the cavaliers who as they dismounted came up to kiss his hand. It was wonderful to see the affability, and the kindness with which he spoke to and embraced them, and the compliments which he made to them.

As he had done so many times before, Cortés triumphed through a skillful combination of courage, trickery, and a magnanimous attitude in victory. Soon virtually all of Narváez' soldiers had become his, and the combined Spanish force was ready to return to Tenochtitlan. On their way back to the Aztec city, Cortés received bad news. Finally, after months of tense coexistence, the Aztecs had risen in force against the Spaniards.

This outbreak of violence can be traced to the decisions and actions of one man: Pedro de Alvarado. During Cortés's absence, Alvarado had kept close to the Spanish quarters and watched Montezuma closely. Although tension was building between the Aztecs and Spaniards, a direct confrontation had been avoided—until the Aztec nobles began to celebrate the festival of Toxcatl.

Held early in June, this festival was the most important of the many that took place during the Aztec calendar year. On this occasion, thousands of the Aztec nobles and warriors entered the courtyard of the Great Temple to take part

vitzilapan.

Since Cortés left Cuba without official sanction, Governor Velasquez sent Pánfilo Narváez and a large group of Spanish soldiers to arrest him. This drawing shows Cortés defeating these soldiers and taking Narváez prisoner.

in a celebration that lasted for days. The Aztec military costumes, which emulated the ferocity of the eagle and the jaguar, were intimidating. Their appearance, along with the tremendous noise of their celebration, made the Spaniards feel threatened. They may have though the Aztecs were going to attack. Whether or not they intended to will never be known, since Pedro de Alvarado struck first.

There were only four doorways into the courtyard of the Great Temple, and Alvarado knew those entrances well. He had all four entrances blocked, and then entered the courtyard with all the men at his disposal. Since there were

The Aztec warriors attacked by Alvardo during the festival of Toxcatl were dressed in their military uniforms, which made them look like jaguars and eagles. Their obsidian knives and swords were no match for the Spaniards superior weaponry.

some sick Spaniards and since some had to be left guarding Montezuma, those who followed Alvarado were probably only 80 in number, but they were in full armor and had the advantage of surprise.

What followed was one of the most ghastly slaughters seen in the history of Tenochtitlan. Over a period of several hours, Alvarado and his men slew thousands of Aztecs. (Estimates by Spanish friars later ran as high as 8,000.) The Aztec warriors were in full military regalia, but the Spanish attack caught them by surprise. As had been the case several times before, the Spanish blades forged in Toledo were too much for the obsidian knives and swords of the Aztecs.

An Aztec account of the attack written many years later ran as follows:

> At this moment in the fiesta, when the dance was loveliest and when song was linked to song, the Spaniards were seized with an urge to kill the celebrants. They all ran forward, armed as if for battle . . . They attacked all the celebrants, stabbing them, spearing them, striking them with their swords. They attacked some of them from behind, and these fell instantly to the ground with their entrails hanging out. Others they beheaded: they cut off their heads, or spilt their heads to pieces.

Alvarado's attack worked to perfection. Thousands of the best Aztec warriors were killed in one afternoon, with only a minimal loss of Spanish lives. However, the actual loss to the Spanish can not be measured in lives, but in diplomacy—the entire population of Tenochtitlan then turned on the Spaniards, forcing them to defend their narrow quarters. Alvarado and his men were trapped inside the great city. This time nothing, not even the diplomatic entreaties of Montezuma or Cortés, would prevent an all-out war between the warriors of Tenochtitlan and the Spanish soldiers.

34 Retirada de
los Españoles la no=
che triste 35 Acclaman
à Quauhtemoc por Rey
36 Guerra en Tacuba, y
queman los Españo
las Cassas.

This painting depicts the Spanish retreat from Tenochtitlan during the Night of Sorrows. The Aztecs were determined to wipe out the Spaniards once and for all, and used the darkness and hand-to-hand combat to their advantage.

The Night of Sorrows: The Spaniards Flee Tenochtitlan

At this moment the trumpets and shouts of the enemy were heard, and the alarm was given by them, crying out, "Taltelulco, Tatelulco, out with your canoes! The Teules are going, attack them at the bridges!"

—Bernal Diaz, *The True History of the Conquest of Mexico*

Cortés returned to Tenochtitlan on the afternoon of June 24, 1520. He came with a much larger force than he had previously: about 1,300 Spaniards and more than 2,000 Tlaxcallan allies. The Spaniards had every reason to feel confident as they approached the city, but the difference between the welcome they received on their return and that which they received on their first arrival in November 1519 could not have been more apparent.

No one met the Spaniards. The streets were empty. There were no bells, no shouts, hardly any noise at all. In the midst of this ominous silence, Cortés and his men made their way to the central part of Tenochtitlan, where they were greeted by Alvarado and the Spaniards who had survived the battle of the courtyard.

Just one day after they entered, Cortés and his men were besieged. The Aztecs came from every direction and attacked the Spaniards in their compound. Cortés now had greater numbers than before, and his men used their crossbows and cannon to deadly effect. However, one of their greatest weapons, the horses, were too large to use in the narrow compound area.

Always inventive, Cortés had two large blockhouses built on wheels. Each of the blockhouses would shelter 24 Spaniards, who could then fire their crossbows or harquebus, a type of large gun, at will on the Aztecs. But the enemy learned of the new inventions and burned them in the night.

At this time Lord Montezuma lost his life. Two conflicting stories about his death started to circulate immediately, and have circulated ever since. The Spaniards claimed that Montezuma was brought forth to beg his people to stop their attacks. This supposedly angered the Aztecs so much that they threw missiles at Montezuma and mortally wounded him. The Aztec story was that the Spaniards decided that Montezuma was no longer of any use and had him strangled. In either case, the chief speaker was dead.

Montezuma had been the eighth chief speaker. As soon as they learned of his death, the Aztec nobles met and proclaimed Cuitlahua as the ninth Aztec leader. Aztec agriculture involved the sale and use of large amounts of human excrement, so it is likely that Cuitlahua, whose name means "excrement-owner," was a merchant. Aztec nobles,

Pedro de Alvarado

Hernán Cortés was the brain and soul of the Spanish conquest, but Pedro de Alvarado was its might and brawn. No other conquistador was so feared and admired by the Aztecs.

Born in Badajoz, Spain, in 1485, Alvarado went to the Caribbean in 1510 and received a grant of land in Cuba the following year. Alvarado was one of the original Spaniards who accompanied Cortés to Mexico in 1519, and he generated controversy from the beginning.

The Totonacs who met Alvarado first were amazed by his physical strength and beauty; they called him "Taino" meaning "The Sun." This admiration turned to fear and hatred when Alvarado was made commander of the small garrison in Tenochtitlan during Cortés's absence. No one knows whether Alvarado acted entirely on his own or whether he had some secret understanding with Cortés, but Alvarado struck the Aztecs while they were in the midst of their great festival. Thousands of Aztec nobles were slain, depriving the Indians of many of their best war leaders.

Though he chastised Alvarado in public, Cortés never removed his lieutenant from positions of leadership. A cult of invincibility had grown up around Alvarado; many of the conquistadors had seen him defy the odds and survive so many times that they wanted to serve with him all the time. Alvarado fueled this myth of invincibility with an amazing pike vault over a chasm on the Night of Sorrows; even today, it is still known as "Alvarado's Leap."

In the final battle for Tenochtitlan, Alvarado led one of the three divisions of the Spanish-Indian army. Although he made some tactical errors, Alvarado was invaluable for his courage and daring; he seemed to instill the same courage in those who followed him.

In 1524 Alvarado led the Spanish invasion of the jungles of Mayan country in what is now Guatemala. His campaign succeeded to such an extent that Mayans today still parade images of Alvarado at festival days, a testament to his infamy among the Mayans.

unlike European nobles, were often businessmen. Cuitlahua was not formally inaugurated until September, and in the interval there was a pause in hostilities as the Aztecs mourned their losses.

Cortés decided that being in Tenochtitlan put his men at a disadvantage. He wanted to get out of the city, where his horses and his Indian allies could be used to greater effect. The great question was: which exit route to take?

There were three causeways leading out of the city. The northern bridge led to Tepeyac, the western bridge led to Tlacopan, and the southern bridge led to Ixtlapalapan. There was also the possibility of taking canoes and fleeing to the east side of the lake, where the Indians of Texcoco were friendly to the Spanish cause. Cortés decided against crossing the lake and in favor of taking the most direct route, across the western causeway. His men and their Indian allies were alerted, and at midnight on the evening of June 30, 1520, Cortés's army began to escape. Bernal Diaz described the departure in his account of the battle:

> A little before midnight the detachment which took charge of the portable bridge set out upon its march, and arriving at the first canal or aperture of water, it was thrown across. The night was dark and misty, and it began to rain. The bridge being fixed, the baggage, artillery, and some of the cavalry passed over it, as also the Tlascalans with the gold. Sandoval and those with him passed, also Cortés and his party after the first and many other soldiers. At this moment the trumpets and shouts of the enemy were heard, and the alarm was given by them, crying out, 'Taltelulco, Tatelulco, out with your canoes! The Teules are going, attack them at the bridges.'

It turned into a night of sheer disaster for the Spaniards. Aztec warriors appeared from every direction, some in canoes, many more on foot. The Aztecs fought with a fierce dedication; they wanted to eradicate the Spaniards once and for all. In the darkness the Spanish guns were of little use; on the narrow causeways the Spanish superiority in

Cortés and his men built wooden blockhouses on wheels, which offered them a protected area from which to fire on the Aztecs. The sheer number of Aztecs fighting in the battle eventually overwhelmed the Spaniards, and they were forced to retreat.

hand-to-hand combat was less decisive. Most important, the Aztecs were present in great numbers, and they never slackened their attack even as the casualties mounted.

Cortés nearly drowned, but was rescued. As the sun rose over the great lake, he and the survivors stood on the west bank, nearly overcome by the Night of Sorrows. Some survivors claimed that Cortés's first question was whether the carpenter of the expedition had survived. This naturally led to other questions: What use would a carpenter be? Was there any further purpose in the Spanish campaign?

Cortés lost about 800 men that night—nearly two-thirds of his entire Spanish force. The loss of his Indian allies was not calculated, but it probably was just as great. Although the Aztecs suffered horribly in the night battle, as well, they had cleansed the city of the foreigners.

Building

The Spaniards fled northeast from Tenochtitlan after the Night of Sorrows, and reached the city of Teotihuacan. This city housed the impressive Pyramid of the Sun, and was also where Montezuma would go to pray and meditate every 20 days.

The early phase of the conquest of Mexico is even more dramatic, more fantastic, because hundreds of miles from the sea a prefabricated navy was built and climactic battle took place on waters that now scarcely exist.

—C. Harvey Gardiner,
Naval Power in the Conquest of Mexico

Cortés and his men, greatly reduced in number, moved north and then east, traveling in a semicircle around Lake Texcoco. To go in any other direction would have invited more attacks. By moving north, he and his few remaining allies were able to regroup.

Teotihuacan

The Battle of Otumba was fought in sight of one of the great architectural marvels of the ancient world. Located just 25 miles northeast of Tenochtitlan, Teotihuacan was known to the Aztecs as "The Place where Men Became Gods."

Archeology now tells us that Teotihuacan was inhabited between about 200 years B.C.E. and 650 C.E. Scholars estimate that between 125,000 and 150,000 people lived in about 2,000 permanent, multifamily apartment compounds. We do not know what language they spoke or the derivation of their ethnicity, but decades of archeological work have convinced many that the people of Teotihuacan had developed a truly advanced form of civilization before the decline and fall of the city. For the Aztecs, who lived just to the southeast, the ruins of Teotihuacan exerted a special fascination, much as Roman ruins would do for generations of medieval Italians.

The chief marvels of Teotihuacan are the Pyramid of the Sun, the Pyramid of the Moon, and the Avenue of the Dead. The Pyramid of the Sun is 216 feet high and measures about 10 acres at its base, making it the largest of all pyramids built in Central or South America. The entire area of the city covers about eight square miles; many of the outlying regions have yet to be excavated.

Many things have yet to be discovered at Teotihuacan, but it is quite possible we will never know how the city came about or what drove the people there to build such masterpieces. It is a reminder, however, that Cortés and the Spaniards stumbled upon a civilization that was much more ancient and venerable than the they first believed.

On July 7, the Spaniards came into sight of one of the greatest marvels of Pre-Columbian America: the Pyramids of the Sun and the Moon at Teotihuacan. These pyramids were so impressive that Montezuma had made a special point of going to Teotihuacan every 20 days during his reign to meditate and pray.

There was no time now, though, to celebrate the

architectural wonders. A very large Aztec army, which some Spaniards claimed numbered 200,000 men, had assembled on the plain to the south. Even if this number was overstated by 90 percent, the Spaniards would still have faced 20,000 Aztecs—a formidable force capable of destroying Cortés and his men.

The battle, called the Battle of Otumba, raged throughout the late morning and into the mid-afternoon. The situation looked desperate for the Spaniards and their Indian allies, but late in the day Cortés spied the leader of the enemy, and rode straight for him with a handful of mounted men:

> The eagle eye of Cortés no sooner fell on this personage than it lighted up with triumph. Turning quickly round to the cavaliers at his side, among whom were Sandoval, Olid, Alvarado, and Avilam, he pointed out the chief, exclaiming, 'There is our mark! Follow and support me!' Then crying his war cry and striking his iron heel into his weary steed, he plunged headlong into the thickest of the press. His enemies fell back, taken by surprise, and daunted by the ferocity of the attack. Those who did not were pierced through with his lance or borne down by the weight of his charger. The cavaliers followed close in the rear. On they swept with the fury of a thunderbolt, cleaving the solid ranks asunder, strewing their path with the dying and the dead, and bounding over every obstacle in their way. In a few minutes they were in the presence of the Indian commander, and Cortés, overturning his supporters, sprang forward with the strength of a lion, and, striking him through with his lance, hurled him to the ground.

The Aztecs turned and ran after their chief was

The Spaniards, buoyed up by Cortés's courage and intensity, were victorious at the Battle of Otumba despite being greatly outnumbered by the Aztecs.

killed. The Spaniards and their allies killed many of the retreating foe, then settled into an exhausted stupor for the night. If they had been expelled from the great city and forced to retreat for their lives, at least they had won this impressive victory under the shadow of the Mexican pyramids.

While they had failed to destroy the Spaniards, the Aztecs celebrated their victory of the Night of Sorrows. Cuitlahua, the new chief speaker, led the celebrations. The hated strangers had been evicted, and the Aztecs could at last devote themselves to rebuilding their city, which bore many signs of the fighting. Within two months of the Spanish departure, however, the Aztecs faced a new enemy: disease. Bernal Diaz described the process:

> Narváez brought with him a Negro who was in the smallpox; an unfortunate importation for that country, for the disease spread with inconceivable rapidity, and the Indians died by thousands; for not knowing the nature of it, they brought it to a fatal issue by throwing themselves into cold water in the heat of the disorder. Thus black was the arrival of Narváez, and blacker still the death of such multitudes, without having an opportunity of being admitted into the bosom of our holy church.

No Spaniards, in fact no Europeans at all, were on hand to witness the death wrought by the smallpox. But given the way smallpox would later move through Indian populations in North America (thousands died in Florida and Alabama after Hernán de Soto passed through in 1538), it seems likely that the Aztec population lost some tens of thousands of people to the epidemic. The rapid spread of the disease and the high mortality rate that accompanied it are not surprising, considering the congested living conditions in Tenochtitlan and the surrounding areas.

Historians have often questioned why the Aztecs did not pursue the defeated Spaniards after the Night of Sorrows. The answer is probably twofold. The Aztecs needed to mourn their dead and consolidate the rule of the new chief speaker. When this was complete, the smallpox epidemic struck, reducing their numbers and willingness to fight.

Because of these factors, Cortés and the remainder of his army were able to round Lake Texcoco and make their way to the capital city of the Tlaxcallans, who remained their closest allies. The defeat during the Night of Sorrows had been bitter, but Cortés was soon able to assure the Tlaxcallan nobles all would be well. The Tlaxcallans might have regretted their alliance with the foreigners, but it was too late to turn back now. If they and the Spaniards failed, it was certain that the Aztecs would exact a frightful revenge. Therefore, the Tlaxcallans listened to Cortés's requests.

Cortés perceived that it would be impossible to take and hold Tenochtitlan by attacking over land alone. The narrow causeways and the congested city streets would render his best weapons less useful. He needed to strike from the water, on Lake Texcoco, as well.

This was almost an entirely new concept to the Tlaxcallans. They were a land-based people, who had very few boats of any kind. The Aztecs were the best at water transport and fighting on the water, but even they were limited to canoes, which formed the basis for transportation around the lake. Now Cortés told the Tlaxcallans his ambitious plans for building a fleet of ships.

No one should have been surprised at his audacity.

Cortés realized that the most-effective attack of Tenochtitlan would come from the water, on Lake Texcoco. The Spaniards and their Indian allies built *brigantines* inland to ensure the element of surprise.

This was the same man who had entered Tenochtitlan at an enormous risk, who had kidnapped Montezuma, defeated Narváez, and was still alive after the Night of Sorrows. Cortés was nothing if not bold and inventive. Cortés surprised the Tlaxcallans when he proposed that they build the boats, (*brigantines* was the Spanish word), in the mountains east of the lake. Cortés wanted to have the advantage of surprise, and he did not want the Aztecs to have any opportunity to attack the ships as they were being built.

Neither Cortés nor his men were natural sailors or shipbuilders. Martin Lopez, the most experienced carpenter among the Spaniards, led the work. He was assisted by a handful of Spaniards who had some experience in woodworking, and by thousands of Tlaxcallans whose labor was donated by their leaders. During the winter months of 1520 to 1521, Martin Lopez, his small group of Spaniards, and his vast numbers of Tlaxcallan laborers, turned out the single biggest surprise of the campaign: ships that were built inland and then pushed, pulled, and dragged down to Lake Texcoco.

At the same time, Cortés undertook a series of campaigns against Aztec towns in the neighborhood of Tlaxcalla. The Aztec army did not stir from Tenochtitlan, probably because of the disarray in the Aztec leadership. Cortés subdued one town after another, and often then turning the town over to his Tlaxcallan allies to sack and burn. The Spaniards taught the Tlaxcallans the slash and burn techniques of European warfare.

The Aztecs did not stir throughout the fall and early winter. Their new leader, Cuitlahua, died around December 5, just three months after he had become the Aztecs' official chief speaker. Unlike the Spaniards, who often came to war decisions through soldiers' councils, the Aztecs were extremely dependent on the leadership of their chief speaker. He had the power to command the armies, and he was responsible for keeping the good will of the gods. Therefore, the loss of Montezuma and Cuitlahua in the same year was much more devastating to the Aztecs than would have been the loss of any of the Spaniards' leaders.

Cuauhtemoc ("He-descends-like-an-eagle") suc- ceeded Cuitlahua as the 10th chief speaker of the Aztec nation. Although he was only 18 years old, Cuauhtemoc had shown more fire and spirit than his fellow Aztec nobles throughout the trials of the past year. Along with Cuitlahua, Cuauhtemoc had urged Montezuma to fight the Spaniards long before they had ever reached Tenochtitlan. In their new chief speaker, the Aztecs had found a warrior worthy of their national spirit.

Cortés, though, was as cunning and dangerous as ever. Not once, in all the trials which had befallen him and his army since the Night of Sorrows, had Cortés shown any sign of abandoning the fight. When his army had reached the safety of the Tlaxcallan towns, many of his soldiers had urged him to flee to Veracruz and return to Cuba if necessary. However, as long as he was their leader, the Spaniards were in Mexico to stay.

The Spaniards fought the Aztecs on the water from the brigantines, and then on the causeways leading to Tenochtitlan. Although the Aztecs fought valiantly, the Spanish eventually defeated them and captured the city.

Broken Spears: The Siege and Destruction of Tenochtitlan

I have read of the destruction of Jerusalem, but I cannot conceive that the mortality there exceeded this of Mexico; for all the people from the distant provinces which belonged to this empire had concentrated themselves here, where they mostly died.

—Bernal Diaz,
The True History of the Conquest of Mexico

The new year dawned for the Spaniards on January 1, 1521. It came about three weeks later for the Aztecs, who began the year Three House on January 24. Three House did not have the sinister applications for the Aztec leadership that the year One

Reed did, and by this point most of the Aztecs had given up the notion that the Spaniards were gods. If they were the representatives of Quetzacoatl, why would they have wrecked such destruction on the land to which their lord intended to return?

Cortés began his new campaign in earnest in the middle part of February. He marched from the Tlaxcallan towns with over 1,000 Spaniards. (Reinforcements had come to him from Cuba in the later part of 1520.) He was also accompanied by over 20,000 Tlaxcallan warriors. When the combined force reached the town of Texcoco, on the eastern bank of the lake, shouts were raised: "Castile! Castile! Tlaxcalla! Tlaxcalla!"

By now the Spaniards and Tlaxcallans had formed a strong and permanent alliance. Many historians criticize the Tlaxcallans for helping Spain to bring down the Aztecs and thereby control all of Mexico, but by this time the Tlaxcallans had no choice. They had been among the first to resist Cortés back in the fall of 1519, and their strength had not prevailed against the Spaniards. At this point they had been in alliance with the foreigners so long that they could not have become the Aztec's allies even if they had wanted to.

Tlaxcallan laborers performed the thankless task of dragging Cortés's ships across a series of low mountains, down to the bank of Lake Texcoco. This was one of the most important aspects of the campaign and a perfect example of Cortés's brilliant skill at improvisation.

The ships were part of the master plan of the Spaniards: to bring Tenochtitlan down through a combination of direct force and envelopment. The brigantines were launched on April 28, and their presence made an immediate impact on Aztec control of the lake.

Martin Lopez, the Spanish carpenter, had done his work well. There were 13 ships in all. Twelve of the ships were of the same size: 42 feet long and 9 feet wide. The 13th, the flagship, was slightly longer at about 49 feet. The ships were built in the Spanish naval tradition, but slightly altered so that they were flat-bottomed. This proved to be an advantage on Lake Texcoco.

By May 1, 1521 Cortés had summoned all his allies. There were others besides the Tlaxcallans, but the Spaniards were confident only in the loyalty of their oldest allies. Cortés's brushes with defeats and his escapes from death had elevated him to a new status with his Indian allies. They did not see him as the returned Quetzacoatl, but they believed he was a new type of man, sent to deliver them from the oppressive tribute system of the Aztecs.

Cortés divided his army into three main columns. Two made direct assaults on the bridge and causeways that led from the mainland to Tenochtitlan. The third, under the leadership of Cortés himself, used the brigantines to attack the Aztec canoe fleets and prevent food from reaching the great city. Cortés had hit upon one of the major weaknesses of the Aztec system. Lacking horses, carts, and even wheels, the Aztecs in Tenochtitlan were extremely dependent on food being delivered to the city on a daily basis. Lake Texcoco was brackish, so even water had to be brought in. All this was made possible through the system of *chinampas* (floating gardens) and the fleet of Aztec canoes. Now Cortés came to challenge Aztec control of the lake.

The siege began in earnest on May 28, when the Spaniards cut the canal from Chaputepec, which brought water to the city. Hoping for a quick kill, Cortés waged an all-out battle in the early days of June, attacking the Aztecs on the causeways and in their canoes. The Spaniards killed thousands of Aztecs, but the Aztecs continued to fight with a determined spirit.

The Aztecs set up pointed stakes in the water around Tenochtitlan, and were able to keep the brigantines at bay. The fighting shifted to the three main causeways into the city, as depicted at the center of this drawing.

Unable to get aboard and capture the brigantines, the Aztecs set up long, pointed stakes at points all around the island, stopping the ships from coming closer. Numerous Aztecs sacrificed their lives in brave attempts to board the ships, but they were thwarted each time by the combination of archers and men in armor. This type of hand-to-hand fighting was a specialty for many of the Spaniards. By contrast, fighting on the water was new for the Aztecs.

The stakes worked well enough, though, in keeping the

ships at bay. The focus of the battle shifted to the three causeways approaching the city, and the battles there were intense. Alvarado could be seen everywhere, exhorting his men, driving his Indian allies forward. But the Aztecs by now had found another weapon; they hurled rocks and stones at the Spaniards, and often enough the missiles found their way into chinks and connection points in the Spanish armor. The ratio of killed and wounded was in favor of the Spaniards to the extreme, but there were Spanish casualties just the same.

Cortés sent numerous messages to the city under flags of truce. All attempts to negotiate were spurned by Cuauhtemoc. The Aztecs also sent messages of their own, directed to the Indian allies of Cortés. The Aztecs predicted correctly that if Cortés were to win the siege, all of Mexico would fall under the control of the conquistadors. Would the other natives not prefer to be ruled by people of their own kind? These messages fell on deaf ears until the Spaniards stumbled badly on June 20.

Cortés remembered the Night of Sorrows well. Therefore, throughout the siege Cortés ordered that his men fight on the causeways and in the city during the day, and return to their own fortified places each night. In the darkness, the Aztecs had out-maneuvered and surrounded many of the Spaniards. Cortés's instructions were usually followed to the letter, but on June 20, Alvarado was given an opportunity which he could not resist. Sensing an Aztec retreat, Alvarado pushed further into the city than usual and was cut off with his advance guard. Through luck and daring, Alvarado escaped with most of his men, but five Spaniards were captured and killed in the most gruesome of fashions. The Aztec chants that night exulted over their success. Some of Cortés's Indian allies began to waver.

By July the Aztecs had withdrawn to the northern

Maria de Estrada

Maria de Estrada was known as the only "conquistadora," a woman who rode, fought, and lived like the male conquistadors.

Very little information about her life can be confirmed but it is possible that she was a Spanish gypsy who traveled to the New World around 1504. (She may have met Cortés on the crossing.) What is certain is that she was with the original group of 600 Spaniards who landed in Mexico in 1519, and that she participated in many of the most dangerous parts of the campaigns that followed.

When Pedro de Alvarado attacked the Aztec nobles in the midst of their dance at the Great Temple, Maria de Estrada was among the conquistadors who rode in and lanced many of the Indians. Some Aztec stories circulated about an apparition of a goddess (perhaps the Virgin Mary), who rode and fought with the men of Spain. Maria fought valiantly in the subsequent battles on the Night of Sorrows and on the Plain at Otumba.

Shortly after the completion of the Spanish conquest, Maria married Pedro Sanchez Farfan, who served as procurator of the new city of Mexico in 1525. They did not have a happy marriage, and after his death in 1538, she married Alonso Martin Partidor. The couple had an estate near the city of Puebla, and there are rumors that they enjoyed a great deal of religious freedom in private. (She was a gypsy; he was a Jew.)

Maria de Estrada died in an epidemic of typhus in 1546, at the age of 64. Though the historical record is far from complete, she remains one of the most compelling figures from Cortés's army.

part of their island, a suburb called Tlatelolco, which had once been a city in its own right. Cortés made almost exactly the same mistake that Alvarado had made, and about 50 Spaniards fell into enemy hands. Cortés himself was stunned and nearly captured, but he was saved by Cristobal de Olea and an unnamed Tlaxcallan. That night the Aztec drums boomed as the 50 Spaniards were sacrificed. The Aztecs burned some of the captives; others were eaten, and pieces of their flesh were hurled at the Spanish outposts. "Eat the flesh of these Teules and of your brothers, for we are already glutted with it!"

Many of Cortés's allies deserted him at this point. These Indians knew the vengeful traits of the Aztecs and had no desire to be on the losing side. But all the Tlaxcallans stuck with Cortés, and within a few days he was again pressing the Aztecs, pushing them until there was nowhere for them to go.

The last days of the siege were the worst. There was no place to put the bodies of those who had been killed; mounds of the dead began to pile up everywhere. The Aztecs fought on, but they had no illusion left, no hope of any sort of victory. The end came on August 13, when Cuauhtemoc fled the island in a canoe. He and his last followers were caught by Sandoval and Garcia Holguin, and the last chief speaker was brought before Cortés. Diaz described the scene:

> The unfortunate monarch, with tears in his eyes, and sinking under affliction, then addressed him in the following words. 'Malinitzin! I have done that which was my duty in the defence of my kingdom and people; my efforts have failed, and being now brought by force a prisoner in your hands, draw that poinard from your side, and stab me to the heart.' Cortés used every expression to comfort him, by assurances that he held him in high esteem for the valour and firmness he had shewn, and that he had required a submission from him and the people at the time that they could no longer reasonably hope for success, in order to prevent further destruction; but that was all past, and no more to be thought of.

The battle for Tenochtitlan was violent, and both sides suffered
many losses. However, the Aztecs were almost completely wiped
out – historians estimate that as many as 250,000 Aztecs were
killed by the Spaniards from 1519-1521.

Cortés's description of the capture of Cuauhtemoc was similar:

> Then he placed his hand upon a dagger of mine and asked me to kill him with it; but I reassured him saying that he need fear nothing. Thus, with this lord a prisoner, it pleased God that the war should cease, and the day it ended was Tuesday, the feast of Saint Hippolytus, the 13th of August in the year 1521. Thus from the day we laid siege to the city, which was on the 30th of May of that same year, until it fell, there passed 75 days, during which time Your Majesty will have seen the dangers, hardships and misfortunes which these, Your vassals, endured, and in which they ventured their lives. To this, their achievements will bear testimony.

The wounded, dead, and dying presented a scene horrible to behold. In his letters to Emperor Charles V, Cortés estimated that some 40,000 Aztecs died in just the last three days of fighting. Sober historical estimates of the total Aztec loss, from 1519 through the end of the siege, run from about 200,000 to 250,000 Aztecs. Given that such a high percentage of the Aztec nobility had died and that their capital was now a smoking ruin, one could say that the Aztec nation had ceased to exist.

New Spain

9

The architecture in modern-day Mexico, the former site of Tenochtitlan, reflects the area's cultural evolution. This picture shows 500 years of Mexican history—Aztec ruins, a colonial church, and modern apartment buildings.

Alien plants grew alongside the old plants in Mexico, and its 1592 fauna, in its large animals, was as different from that of 1492 as the native fauna of Zimbabwe differs from that of Spain.

—Herman J. Viola and Carolyn Margolis,
Seeds of Change

A nation was dead, and a new colony and a new people quickly took its place. There was no more resistance to the conquistadors. Their Indian allies, who outnumbered them by at least fifty-to-one, meekly accepted the small rewards handed them by Cortés and went home. The siege, the battle, and the war were all over, and the Spaniards had won one of the most decisive conflicts yet seen in human history. What would they do with their victory?

Ever ambitious, Cortés sent out small groups of Spaniards to explore, and where necessary, to subjugate Indians in a 200-mile radius of Tenochtitlan. There was little need for fighting; the reputation of the Spaniards preceded them, and most natives professed themselves to be subjects of Cortés and Emperor Charles.

Cortés also looked to rebuild Tenochtitlan. In the aftermath of the battle, he and the Spaniards removed themselves and let the Aztec survivors deal with the dead, the dying, and the rubble that had been created by the siege. Once the rubble had been cleared enough to consider rebuilding, Cortés decided that the area would be reclaimed as the Spanish capital and renamed the City of Mexico. He wrote to Emperor Charles V:

> As I always wished the great city to be rebuilt because of its magnificent and marvelous position, I strove to collect together all the inhabitants who, since the war, had fled to other parts . . . I have always tried to honor and favor them, and they have done so well that now there are some 30,000 people living in the city, and the markets and commerce are organized as before. I have given them such liberties and exemptions that the population grows each day, for they live very comfortably and many of the artisans live by working among the Spaniards: these are carpenters, masons, stone cutters, silversmiths, and others. The merchants carry on their business in full confidence, and the other people live either by fishing, which is a flourishing trade in this city, or by agriculture, for many of them have their own plantations where they grow all the vegetables grown in

Spain of which we have been able to obtain seeds. I assure Your Caesarean Majesty that if they could but be given plants and seeds from Spain, and if Your Highness were pleased to command them to be sent to us, as I requested in my earlier report, there would in a very short time be a great abundance of produce, for these Indians are much given to cultivating the soil and planting orchards.

The plants and seeds came. Within 50 years of the Spanish conquest, Mexico was transformed into a land where the flora and fauna resembled those of Spain. Citrus trees flourished; ranches were created; pigs and cattle were seen everywhere. Although the Spaniards initially maintained a law which forbade natives to ride horses, Indians found a way around the law, and the Mexican *vaquero* (cowboy) became renowned.

In their book *Seeds of Change*, Herman J. Viola and Carolyn Margolis speculate about what the Aztec chief speaker Ahuitzotl might have found if he had been able to return to Mexico in 1592, 100 years after Columbus began the Spanish penetration of the Western Hemisphere:

If Lord Ahuitzotl had returned to Mexico (now New Spain) a hundred years after 13-Flint he would have found much the same as in his lifetime. He would have recognized the profiles of the mountains, all the wild birds, and most of the plants. The basic and holy food of his people was still maize. But he would have been stunned by the sight of plants and creatures he had never seen or dreamed of during his days on earth. Alien plants grew alongside the old plants in Mexico, and its 1592 fauna, in its large animals, was as different from that of 1492 as the native fauna of Zimbabwe differs from that of Spain.

Maize, Chilies, and Chocolate

Cortés and his fellow Spaniards wanted gold and silver from the Aztecs, but the Spanish conquest brought other, more-valuable products to Europe.

Maize (corn) was the major reason the Aztec people were able to support such a large city as Tenochtitlan. The crop yielded a higher caloric and protein count than most of the Old World crops, such as wheat and barley. It took nearly 200 years, but maize eventually became one of the staple crops of Europe, especially in hilly areas such as northern Italy and the Balkans.

Chilies were used throughout the Aztec lands. They provided a rich flavoring that enhanced many European dishes. Chilies became mainstays in the diets of the Italians and other Mediterranean peoples.

Chocolate became one of the great gifts of the Aztecs to the rest of the world. Chocolate had been a delicacy of the Aztec upper classes and had been included in the tribute paid by many subject peoples.

Chocolate passed to Europe from Mexico via the Caribbean Islands. Cultural historians note that chocolate and sugar are nearly universally appealing; very few cultures once exposed to these tastes have ever abandoned them. As a result, the race to profit from sugar production in the Caribbean Islands started the Spanish conquest of Mexico.

Cortés had conquered every battlefield foe, but he still had some cause for concern. With the exception of his legal fiction, created at the city of Villa Rica de la Vera Cruz, Cortés had been an outlaw since the time he left Cuba in February 1519. He still did not know the attitude of Emperor Charles V.

A great amount of the Spanish treasure had been lost when his men tried to carry it out of the city on the Night of Sorrows. (Very little of that gold and silver was ever found again.) After Tenochtitlan fell, Cortés set about

Cortés and the Spaniards lost most of the treasure they had horded when they had to flee on the Night of Sorrows. However, the Mexican conquest had added land to the Spanish Empire, which pleased Charles V. Cortés was rewarded, but his soldiers did not fare as well.

collecting treasure once more, but what he found was not even half as much as had been seen in the glorious days when Montezuma had welcomed him to the city. Dutifully, Cortés shepherded the "king's fifth" and sent it to Spain.

The treasure never arrived at Seville. Instead, the Spanish ships were captured by five French privateers, and the gold and silver wound up enriching King Francis I, who was one of Charles V's most implacable enemies.

Despite this setback, Cortés did well at the court of Spain. Charles V was notoriously short of money, and the news that Cortés had added an enormous section of land across the world to his empire was welcome. It took about two more years for the formalities to be concluded, but Cortés was made the Marques de Valle of Oaxaca and given the title of captain-general of New Spain.

His lieutenants did not fare as well. Charles V left the disposition of land and titles to Cortés's discretion, and Cortés was not very generous towards his own men. Few of them profited in the manner they might have expected.

The average soldier fared even worse. One estimate is that the horsemen who survived the expedition and the siege received about 100 gold pesos for their trials— an amount worth about one-fifth the price of a horse. Needless to say, the common infantrymen received even less.

This was pitifully small reward to show for the labors and trials they had endured. Many of the soldiers turned to ranching in the years that followed, and a large number of ranches and plantations sprang up around Mexico.

Bernal Diaz, who must have been possessed of a remarkable memory, wrote many years later about most of the conquistadors. A brief passage from his work indicates the type of men they were, as he perceived them, and the various ends to which they came:

> J. de Esclanate was a captain; he died at Villa Rica. F. de Lugo, a brave officer, acted as captain occasionally; he was the natural son of a wealthy gentleman at medina del Campo; he died a natural death. Gregorio de Monjaraz; a good soldier; lost his hearing during the siege, and died a natural death. Four brothers of Don P., de Alvarado. J. Xaramillo was an officer of merit; he died a natural death. Christoval Flores, a worthy soldier. One Calcedo, a wealthy man. Francisco de Bonal, a good soldier. Maldonado, surnamed 'the broad,' a good soldier. Francisco Alvarez Chico, a man of business. Francisco de Torrazas, major domo to Cortés, a person of merit. Christoval del Corral, our ensign, an officer of merit. Anthonio de Villaroel, some time ensign. Alonzo de Grad; one fitter for business than war; by his importunities he induced Cortés to give him the daughter of Montezuma in marriage. Francisco Flores, a very noble person. De Soils. There were four of this name; one was surnamed 'casquette,' or 'rattle-skull,' another called himself 'De la Huerta,' but we called him 'silk coat,' because he prided himself on his dress.

What became of Cortés and Malinali?

The first is easier to ascertain. Cortés served as the first captain-general of New Spain from 1522 until 1528 when he returned to Spain. During his brief time as the ruler of Mexico, Cortés showed the same sterling qualities that had made him a remarkable military leader. Because of his conquest, a legend had grown up around him, and while he governed the colony, the Indians were entirely quiescent. Cortés also led a daring, and unnecessary, expedition to the

Bay of Honduras. Many valiant exploits were reported, but the sufferings and tribulations of the men who served there were fruitless. Cortés would have done better to spend that same energy in governing Mexico.

When Cortés returned to Spain in 1528, much was made of his arrival. He was praised in every town he passed through, and the celebrations culminated in a magnificent reception given by the emperor, Charles V. Charles gave Cortés the title of Marque de Valle and showed every indication of his royal favor.

As the years passed, Cortés became more of a nuisance than an asset to the Court of Spain. In 1541 he accompanied the emperor on an invasion of Algiers in North Africa, but the campaign came to naught, and Cortés earned no further glories in Spain or the Mediterranean. Although he was officially a man of high standing, Cortés found himself increasingly ostracized as the years passed. He died of a stroke at the estate of the Duke of Medina-Sidonia in 1547.

Cortés's bones were brought from Spain to Mexico City in 1565. His remains were interred at the College of Jesus. One of the few portraits of the conqueror is still hanging in that college.

Malinali's story is less documented. She had been Cortés's mistress as well as his interpreter, and she had given Cortés a son named Martin. The son spent the second half of his life in Spain and was a gentleman in waiting during the wedding between Queen Mary ("Bloody Mary") of England and Prince Philip of Spain.

A very touching story is told by Bernal Diaz of Malinali. As the Spanish army marched on its campaign toward Guatemala, Bernal Diaz relates that the army came to the very town in which Malinali was born. (There is considerable controversy as to what Indian town this was and whether anything of it remains.)

Naturally, the mother and stepfather who sold her into

slavery were alarmed. Their daughter now held great power as the mistress of Cortés and an interpreter for the army. But according to Diaz, Malinali told them to put their fears to rest. She assured them that she believed all was well, that their abandonment of her had been to a good purpose, that it had led her to the Spaniards and therefore to the Christian faith. Malinali took no revenge upon the family which had treated her so badly.

Malinali has not fared well in historical memory. Her nickname "Malinche" has come to mean a Mexican who loves his or her country so little that he or she prefers foreign influence, even foreign domination. It all seems a great burden to place on a 15-year-old girl who had been cast out by her family and handed as a slave to the conquistadors.

Men, Gods, Animals, and Weapons: The Spanish Conquest in the Light of Western Military Tradition

The Spanish were outnumbered by the Aztecs, but were able to capture Tenochtitlan with a relatively small loss of life. Cortés owed this victory to superior weaponry, the use of horses, and Montezuma's inability to act quickly.

The West has achieved military dominance in a variety of ways that transcend mere superiority in weapons and has nothing to do with morality or genes. The Western way of war is so lethal precisely because it is so amoral—shackled rarely by concerns of ritual, tradition, religion, or ethics, by anything other than military necessity.

—Victor Davis Hanson, *Carnage and Culture*

It has been nearly 500 years since Cortés, the Spaniards, and their Indian allies took Tenochtitlan, but the siege and the Spanish conquest remain topics of lively debate. How on earth did something like 1,000 Spaniards overturn an empire with hundreds of thousands of people and some 370 towns that paid tribute?

The answers are multi-layered. First, and perhaps foremost, Montezuma did not respond to the Spanish threat early on because he seems to have believed the Spaniards were representatives of Quetzacoatl. This permitted Cortés and his men to enter Tenochtitlan and see for themselves the vast treasures of the Aztec empire.

The Spaniards and the Aztecs also had very different military traditions. The Aztec style of fighting centered on stunning their opponents and taking them captive, to be sacrificed by the Aztec priests later on. By contrast, the Spanish system of fighting evolved over centuries of war against the Moors and centered on killing their enemies outright with a swift stab of their steel blades. The Aztec empire, prior to the arrival of the Spaniards, had flourished through a combination of terror and the exaction of tribute, while the Spanish conquest of the Moors had meant exile or extermination of the latter.

The Spaniards also held in their hands far better tools of war. Manufactured in Toledo, Spanish steel was the best of its kind in Europe, and even the worst of European blades were superior to the obsidian and flint weapons employed by the Aztecs. In hand-to-hand fighting, the Spaniards would nearly always prevail because of their swords and lances.

Whether they gradually enveloped their enemies' towns and cities or defeated them outright on the battlefield, the Aztecs were always able to use size to their advantage. However, sheer numbers could not help them against the Spaniards' superior weaponry and fighting style.

The Spaniards also had the advantage of horses, which the Aztecs had never seen before. Whenever the Spanish and Aztecs fought on an open field, the Spaniards won because a small row of charging men

Although Cortés's ingenuity and boldness helped the Spanish capture Tenochtitlan, historians believe a similar victory may have been achieved under another leader. Unlike the Aztecs, the Spanish did not rely on one person to make every military decision.

and horses could terrify and scatter large numbers of Indians. Only on the causeways and in the narrow streets of Tenochtitlan were the Aztecs able to thwart the use of horses, and there Cortés found a remedy: he demolished blocks of buildings so that the horses could have free play.

The Aztec leadership was too highly-centralized to allow quick, or dissenting, opinions to be made. When Montezuma was taken hostage by Cortés, the Aztecs could not respond to the situation. He was their chief speaker, and no one even thought about trying to replace him until Alvarado massacred the Aztec nobles in the temple square. By then it was too late.

Although most historians credit the speed of the Spanish victory to Cortés's boldness, ingenuity, and improvisation, the Spanish conquest may well have succeeded under other leadership. The Spaniards had a looser structure of command, supplemented by occasional councils of war in which the average soldier could speak. Bernal Diaz wrote his *The True History of the Conquest of Mexico* to refute the idea that it was Cortés and Cortés alone who performed valiant feats. Diaz emphasizes that Cortés was better described as the "first among equals," and had to cajole and persuade his men to accompany him and to follow his lead. As we know, Cortés was one of the most adept speakers and persuaders the world has ever seen.

The Spanish were outnumbered by the Aztecs, but were able to capture Tenochtitlan with a relatively small loss of life. Cortés owed this victory to superior weaponry, the use of horses, and Montezuma's inability to act quickly.

There will always be some mystery concerning the conquest of Mexico. Was it the belief that the Spaniards may have been gods that kept the Aztecs from attacking earlier? Or was it the presence of horses and dogs which created terror among the Indians? Whatever answer is presented will have its supporters and its detractors. What remains, though, is the remarkable and terrible story of a small band of Spanish adventurers who destroyed a nation and subdued its people in the space of two years and five months.

1325	Aztec people settle on the island which they call Tenochtitlan
1467	Montezuma born
1469	Isabela of Castile and Ferdinand of Aragon marry, bringing a close connection between their two realms
1485	Hernán Cortés born in Medellin, Estramadrura, Spain
1492	The Moorish Kingdom of Granada surrenders to Ferdinand and Isabela, completing the reunification of Spain
1492	Christopher Columbus sails west and arrives in the Bahamas
1500	Charles Habsburg born in Belgium
1502	Montezuma takes the Aztec throne
1504	Cortés crosses the ocean; he stays first in Jamaica, then settles in Cuba
1505	Malinali born in what is now southeast Mexico
1516	Charles Habsburg becomes King of Spain

1325
Aztec people settle on the island which they call Tenochtitlan

1467
Montezuma born

1469
Isabela of Castile and Ferdinand of Aragon marry, bringing a close connection between their two realms

1300 1400

1485
Hernán Cortés born in Medellin, Estramadrura, Spain

1492
The Moorish Kingdom of Granada surrenders to Ferdinand and Isabela, completing the reunification of Spain

Timeline

1519

February 22   Cortés's fleet leaves Santiago, Cuba

April 22   Cortés meets Tentlil, an Aztec governor of the Totanoc people

June 28   Cortés founds Villa Rica de la Vera Cruz; Charles I of Spain wins election as Charles V, Holy Roman Emperor

November 8   Cortés and Montezuma meet for the first time, in Tenochtitlan

November 16   Cortés takes Montezuma as an unofficial prisoner

1520

June 24   Cortés, the Spaniards, and their allies return to Tenochtitlan

June 30   The Spaniards flee Tenochtitlan, the Night of Sorrows

July 7   Battle of Otumba fought near pyramids of Teotihuacan

September 20   Cuitlahauc, the chief speaker, inaugurated

December 5   Cuitlahauc dies of smallpox

February 22, 1519
Cortés's fleet leaves
Santiago, Cuba

April 22, 1519
Cortés meets Tentlil,
a Totanoc governor

May 30, 1521
The siege of
Tenochtitlan
begins

1502
Montezuma takes
the Aztec throne

June 28, 1519
Cortés founds Villa Rica de la
Vera Cruz; Charles I of Spain
wins election as Charles V,
Holy Roman Emperor

August 13, 1521
The last Aztecs
die or surrender;
the siege is over

1500

November 8, 1519
Cortés and Montezuma
meet for the first time,
in Tenochtitlan

June 24, 1520
Cortés, the
Spaniards, and
their allies return
to Tenochtitlan

July 7, 1520
Battle of Otumba fought near
pyramids of Teotihuacan

November 16, 1519
Cortés takes Montezuma
as an unofficial prisoner

June 30, 1520
The Spaniards flee
Tenochtitlan, the
Night of Sorrows

1521

May 30	The siege of Tenochtitlan begins
August 13	The last Aztecs die or surrender; the siege is over
1524	Cortés invades Honduras
1525	Cuauntemoc executed
1528	Cortés returns to Spain; Juan de Zumarraga arrives as the first bishop of Mexico City
1529	Malinali dies
1531	Miracle of Guadalupe takes place
1535	Antonio de Mendoza becomes the first viceroy of New Spain
1541	Cortés accompanies Charles V in his attack on the Moorish city of Algiers
1547	Cortés dies at the estate of the Dukes of Medina-Sidonia
1556	Charles V abdicates his throne and titles
1558	Charles V dies at Yuste, Spain
1632	Bernal Diaz' *The True History of the Conquest of Mexico* is published for the first time

Bernal Diaz del Castillo. *The True History of the Conquest of Mexico*, Written in 1568 by Captain Bernal Diaz del Castillo, one of the conquerors, and translated from the original Spanish by Maurice Keating Esq. London, 1800.

Brading, D.A. *Mexican Phoenix: Our Lady of Guadalupe: Image and Tradition across Five Centuries.* Cambridge University Press, 2001.

Cerwin, Herbert. *Bernal Diaz: Historian of the Conquest.* University of Oklahoma Press, 1963.

Cortés, Hernán. *Letters from Mexico*, edited and translated by Anthony Pagden. Yale University Press, 1986.

Duran, Gloria. *Maria de Estrada: Gypsy Conquistadora.* Latin American Literary Review Press, 1999.

Gardiner, C. Harvey. *Naval Power in the Conquest of Mexico.* University of Texas Press, 1956.

Gomara, Francisco Lopes de. *Cortés: The Life of the Conqueror by His Secretary,* Translated and edited by Lesley Byrd Simpson. University of California Press, 1964.

Hanson, Victor Davis. *Carnage and Culture: Landmark Battles in the Rise of Western Powe.* Doubleday, 2001.

Hassig, Ross. *Time History and Belief in Aztec and Colonial Mexico.* University of Texas Press, 2001.

Hassig, Ross. *Mexico and the Spanish Conquest.* Longman, 1994.

Innes, Hammond. *The Conquistadors.* Alfred A. Knopf, 1969.

Lanyon, Anna. *Malinche's Conquest.* Allen & Unwin, 1999.

Le Clezio, J.M.G. *The Mexican Dreams: Or, The Interrupted Thought of Amerindian Civilizations*. Translated by Teresa Lavender Fagan. Chicago: University of Chicago Press, 1993.

Lockhart, James, editor and translator. *We People Here: Nahuatl Accounts of the Conquest of Mexico.* University of California Press, 1993.

Padden, R.C. *The Hummingbird and the Hawk: Conquest and Sovereignty in the Valley of Mexico, 1503-1541.* Ohio State University Press, 1967.

Leon-Portilla, Miguel, editor. *The Broken Spears: The Aztec Account of the Conquest of Mexico.* Beacon Press, 1962.

Prescott, William H. *History of the Conquest of Mexico, with a Preliminary View of the Ancient Mexican Civilization, and the Life of the Conqueror, Hernán Cortés.* J.B. Lippincott & Co., 1874.

Rodriguez, Dr. Gustavo A. *Dona Marina*. Imprenta de la Secretaria de Relaciones Exteriores, 1935.

Thomas, Hugh. *Conquest: Montezuma, Cortés, and the Fall of Old Mexico*. Simon and Schuster, 1993.

SAMUEL WILLARD CROMPTON teaches both American history and Western Civilization at Holyoke Community College in Massachusetts. Mr. Crompton is the author or editor of many books, among them are *100 Battles that Shaped World History* and *100 Military Leaders Who Shaped World History*. He earned a certificate in Historic Conservation at the restored Fortress of Louisbourg, Nova Scotia in 1997. He has twice served as a Writing Fellow for Oxford University Press in the production of the 24-volume *American National Biography*.